Careering
with Steam

Careering
with Steam

Arthur Turner

Millstream Books

to my wife
and all the other wives of railway shift workers
in appreciation for the devotion they showed
in performing the arduous and often lonely tasks
(especially at night and holiday times)
in order to run the household while their partners were
providing transport to supply the needs of the community.

First published 1996
by Millstream Books, 18 The Tyning, Bath BA2 6AL

Set in 11 point Palatino
Printed in Great Britain by The Amadeus Press, Huddersfield

ISBN 0 948975 44 X

© Arthur Turner 1996

Introduction

For over 100 years the railways of this country had been the main carrier of the country's traffic, both passenger and goods alike. Through progress and development of the passenger and goods rolling stock and the locomotives, the system had been improved beyond recognition. Instead of being small, weak, and unreliable, and only able to run short distances, it was now very reliable and able to pull heavy loads and to run great distances if required. The reliability of these very much larger engines was second to none, so much so that these, or modifications of these steam engines, were used until the 1950s to pull the majority of trains. But gradually steam was phased out and replaced by other means of traction. To see a steam locomotive at the head of a train, whether it was on a passenger train, a goods train, or even a light engine, was a grand sight. So too the sound of an engine whistle as it came near and sought to attract attention of its presence, and to warn everyone to stand clear, or with whistles (often in code) relaying information to railway staff about the job. Maybe it would be relaying "routeing" information, or acknowledging a signal from the signalman. This, with the noise and smell of the engine exhaust steam, sometimes very loud and mixed with any firebox smoke, as it was forced out of the chimney, characterised the steam days. The sound of the wheels as they passed over crossings and rail joints was also a noticeable feature with its "tappity-tap" sound. This, along with the sight of the wheels and connecting rods whirling around as the train proceeded along the track, was a daily scene until a few years ago.

Now that this has given way to progress of a more modern type of traction, to those of us who have witnessed these scenes it remains in our memories as a never-to-be-forgotten sight, which I am sorry to say, will never return.

These times for a footplate man were often difficult and hard work. There were many times when I have got to the end of a journey with a soaking shirt, and an aching body, having been thrown about the footplate by a lurching engine, and having shovelled several tons of coal through the firehole in my endeavour to get the steam required during the day's work. Many books have been written about the railways of these times, and no doubt many more will follow. This is a subject that is very popular with both young and old alike. Amongst the books that I have read there are but a few that tell the inside story of the work of the Locomotive Department where everyone had their individual task for attention to the locomotives, and with a combined effort kept these steeds in good condition and able to go out and do the job that was awaiting them.

Now that I have retired after 47 years of railway work I have been asked to recall some of the things that came my way during my employment on the job. I would like to point out that any of the things that I recall, or similar events, happened to many of the thousands of locomen who were employed on steam locomotives. Maybe many other stories could be told, but my recollections should give a fair description of the work involved in the days of steam.

From Bar Boy to Spare Fireman

Radstock, a small town in the Somerset coalfield, where I lived during my later school days, often came to a halt on the highway for the passage of traffic and pedestrians alike by the closing of the level crossing across the road by the two railways to allow trains to proceed.

Both the GWR and the S&DJR served the town. Each had its own system, and their tracks passed over the main road within 200 yards of each other. Each railway had its own set of crossing gates which were controlled from its own signalbox. These bisected the town, and when one or both sets of gates were set to allow trains through, pedestrians and road traffic alike came to a halt.

The GWR line ran between Frome and Bristol and was usually worked by a tank engine hauling a two-coach set on the passenger service, and a 0-6-0 tender engine was usually on the goods service.

The S&D passenger trains were usually hauled by a 4-4-0 tender engine, although sometimes it was a tank engine of the 0-4-4 type. The goods trains were usually formed of coal wagons, loaded or empty, and various types of tank wagons containing tar or petrol. There were also box vans containing various crates, or sacks of goods; also there were sheeted wagons, and special wagons with long loads of timber or machinery. Many of the empty coal wagons were going back to their owners' sidings or to the various coalmines for refilling. Usually hauling these trains were the large 2-8-0 7F engines which were, when on a southbound train, always impressive with steam often blowing from their safety valves, and with their large boilers and the outside valve gear arrangement making them look like heavy cart-horses waiting to take the strain at their harness when the banker was ready to assist them to haul the train up the bank to Masbury by pushing at the rear.

On leaving school during the summer of 1935, I applied for a job on the railway, but there were no vacancies. Work was not easy to obtain in those days and many of my school chums became employed at the coalmines. It was during this period that my father met with a fatal accident at the locomotive shed at Radstock.

I was able to get a junior job as an assistant on a motor van delivering bread, but this job was for a junior only and with little prospects of an adult position when I became 18 years of age. Eventually I was told of a vacancy on the railway. I applied and was successful.

This position was that of a junior porter at Bath (Green Park) with the LMSR. From the start I did not care for this position. It was a split turn of duty starting at 6.40am, then after six hours to book off only to return during the afternoon for two hours to help with the parcels traffic. This meant a 12-hour day to do an 8-hour turn of duty. It also seemed that I was expected to do other jobs outside of my own rostered work.

My job should have been that of a number taker for the Railway Clearing House of any passenger stock which did not belong to the LMSR that came through Bath, and report this on a weekly return basis, also to assist with parcels traffic. When off duty the foreman dealt with the noting of the stock. I was also rostered for a couple of other duties, but when it came to doing jobs which I knew were rostered to other staff I objected. When I pointed these things out to the foreman things soon changed. All this, along with the fact that I wanted more interesting work than what would be offered in any position in this department in future years, made me look further afield.

I had a conversation with a footplate crew who advised me to apply for a transfer into the Locomotive Department. I applied for a transfer and eventually this was granted. I was told to report to the office at the loco shed to get my instructions as to when I was to start, and what job I was to do.

While I was walking along the path to the loco office there was a crash and I saw more action than I had seen since I started on the railway. The tender of an engine came through the end of the wooden shed just in front of where I was walking. Afterwards I was told that the engine was low in steam pressure and was unable to stop when the brake was applied. Thinking that this was a more interesting job than what I had been doing I was in good spirits when I reported to the Chief Clerk.

He told me that I was to become a bar boy and that I was to clean fireboxes. There was a vacancy in a one of the three shed staff gangs as this bar boy had attained the age of 18 and was due to go into the cleaning gang and get passed out for spare firing duties.

As they were on the night turn starting on Monday 5th July 1937 at 10-00pm, I was to report to the foreman at that time to be trained and to take over from the bar boy in that gang. When a junior cleaner was employed, under the age of 18, he was employed either as a bar boy, or a call boy if there was a vacancy.

A bar boy was put into a shed staff gang under the direction of the steam raiser and cleaned fireboxes and replaced fire-bars as required and worked the 10.00pm to 6.00am, 6.00am to 2.00pm and 2.00pm to 10.00pm shifts on a rotating weekly basis with the other shed staff gangs. The call boys worked mostly at night calling the train crews to make ensure that they were available and not late for work.

Arriving for the night shift I was put in touch with the bar boy and steam raiser. The other members of the gang were the boiler-washer, the tube-cleaner, the ash-pit cleaner and the coalman. Besides cleaning fireboxes on hot and cold engines, the job was to make coal available for the steam raiser's needs in his duties of attending to locomotives needed for service.

At that time the locos were coaled when they were being prepared for service, so the coal used in the lighting up and getting the amount of fire required for the preparing fireman had to be obtained from what was left from the proceeding trip, or obtained by the bar boy.

All engines that were being reserviced had to have their tube-plates cleaned and the fire-grate inspected so as to be in a perfect condition with no fire-bars missing or misplaced.

When engines had been stopped for boiler washing-out, general repairs or just because they hadn't been used for a while, the firebox would have to be cleaned from the inside.

This meant that the bar boy had to get in through the fire-hole feet first and with head downwards, then with special tools clean the firebox of all rubbish that could not readily be done from the outside. All fire-bars would have to be examined and changed, if necessary. This task was one of the least pleasant as it was a very dirty, hot and unthankful job. When all was in order the coal would have to be brought forward for lighting up by the steam raiser. Of course if any fire-bars had to be changed then these would have to be got from the stores pound, and the old ones taken to the scrap bin. No help was given in this direction. All this was hard work for a young lad, but it was taken as part of the job, and a good basic training for future days.

In fact I did have cause to use the knowledge that I gained during my shed days on several occasions later on, and was able to sort things out and put the faults right. The two years that I spent with the shed staff team gave me a chance to watch all the other members of the team doing their work.

One thing that intrigued me was how the boiler-washer set about his task of removing and replacing mud-hole doors and inspection covers, where the rims were larger than the hole which they sealed. They were elliptical, and had to be manipulated into position to make their water-tight seal fit. This I always thought, was a work of art to get them into a position to be a perfect fit.

When the fitters were at work I always, if possible, used to watch how they performed, from a safe distance, and I gained many a useful tip on what was taking place.

Bath LMSR was originally built by the Midland Railway as the terminus of a branch line from Mangotsfield on the main line between Bristol and Gloucester. No doubt it was only intended to be a connection to and from the Midlands and the North. Some while later the S&DJR arrived in Bath and connected with this line at Bath Junction (about a mile west of the passenger station). Both these railways used the same passenger and goods depots and transferred their passenger and goods traffic from one to the other. The S&D built its own loco shed and both companies were run as separate concerns, although they used the same track.

When the LMSR was formed, they were amalgamated and worked as one unit. As time went by, and it was found that more through passenger trains to and from the S&D and the Midlands were required then, as Bath was a terminal station, by putting an engine or engines onto the other end of the incoming train while station work was being done, this same train, although reversed, would be free to carry on to its destination without transfer or delay. There was soon a through service put into operation. In 1927 a service known as the Pines Express was introduced; this was a through train to and from Bournemouth and the North.

When holidays at the seaside became popular, trains from the Midlands and the North were soon making their way via Bath to the South Coast at Bournemouth. Although these trains were well patronised and were loaded to 12 coaches in length, it was not until the end of 1937 that any of the larger types of engines which were now being built to replace the old Midland types were allowed over the Mangotsfield branch to Bath owing to the bridges on this line being unable to take the extra weight of these engines.

Meanwhile these holiday trains had to be content to have a pair of 2P 4-4-0 of the 500 or 600 Class engines to and from the Midlands, and a 4F 0-6-0, with a 2P 4-4-0 assisting, from Bath to Bournemouth and back.

The engines from the Midlands, in any case, were often in need of reservicing, so these engine changes at Bath were very often a blessing in disguise. The engines that took the trains forward were the usual types as used every day on the S&D and were combined to pull the weight of the train and to be able to combat the gradients of the S&D better. They also carried tablet exchangers to exchange the single-line tokens on the several sections which existed at certain places (all except one on the southern section), while travelling at speeds of up to 60mph.

The assisting engines over the S&D had to go through to Bournemouth at that time owing to the bank at Parkstone being too severe for a 4F 0-6-0 with a load of 12 coaches. The Pines was normally booked a 2P for its 6-coach load. If above that limit it was given another 2P for assistance. The up Pines in late 1937 and early 1938 was, for a long time, worked by engine No.601, and the down Pines had engine No.600. The spare engine was No.602 should either of these engines not be available.

Branksome men worked the up Pines to Bath and were relieved to return to Bournemouth working the 1-10pm passenger. Bath men worked the down Pines and returned from Bournemouth working the Last Up passenger from Bournemouth with the same engine. No.601, after working the up Pines was reserviced and returned to Bournemouth on the 6-35pm passenger for the Pines the next day.

When an S&D 7F was required at Derby workshops, it was towed light engine, with the coupling rods disconnected and placed onto the tender, and taken at a reduced speed over the bridges on the Mangotsfield branch, en route for repairs at the factory.

The goods service at Bath LMS did not alter throughout the year, but should there be a build-up of traffic then the Control would ask the Locomotive Department if an engine and men could be found so that a special goods could be run. These extra trains, when required, were run at 5-00am, 7-15am, 2-00pm, or 7-15pm. The footplate men booking on near to this time would be spilt up if the fireman was "passed for driving" and allowed to drive a train over the route. Both men would be given a passed cleaner as a fireman, to crew these trains. The guard was arranged by the Control.

Very little changed in the normal daily passenger service either, except that in the summer service there would be a couple of extra semi-fast trains starting from Bristol and going through to Bournemouth and returning later in the day. This was from Monday to Saturday.

The usual summer service of weekend holiday trains would start off with the Pines, in both up and down directions, running in two parts on Fridays. On Saturdays it would run, in both up and down directions, in four parts.

The Saturday holiday specials would begin to arrive from the North as early as 1-25am in the peak period, and continue to arrive every 15 minutes or so until about 4-15am. These trains, except for the 2.40am Mail from Bath to Bournemouth which ran daily, took up the whole single-line section between Bath and Midford. All the trains, both in and out of Bath, were double-headed.

As the engines from the Midlands came onto the loco they were disposed of and serviced, then they were stabled either in the loco or on the goods line and sidings towards Bath Junction to await their return trains to the Midlands which was towards mid-morning. As soon as this onslaught was completed the next rush would be getting close. The local service would have to be dealt with between these times, and the returning goods trains from the Friday night S&D workings were brought into Bath over the single-line section from Midford to Bath, having been blocked back while the specials were running, when space was available.

When the next rush started the trains from both the S&D and the Midlands converged on Bath at the same time. This was due at about 10-00am and did not stop until about 3-30pm.

There were no spare moments to be taken by anyone, no spare engines anywhere, and some engines could be seen to be having workers doing their tasks, either disposing, preparing, fitters working, or shed staff doing their work, all at the same time. With the last of this rush came a sigh of relief; this was felt by everyone, with the satisfaction of knowing that another Saturday had been successfully dealt with.

This was not the end as there were still the empty stock trains to arrive from Bournemouth, and the 7-50pm and the 10-30pm goods to Templecombe and back, also the 9-15pm, Birmingham goods and the 11-29pm Westerleigh goods to be made available. Then of course the usual local passenger service engines would be arriving at the end of their day's work.

Manning these extra summer trains, and the extra engines required to haul them was a problem. There were several Locomotive Departments on the LMS that consisted of all goods and coal work. These depots were not fully used during the summer period as coal trains were required less at power stations and domestic fuel suppliers. Their spare engines were often 4F 0-6-0s and were just the type that Bath required. These depots wished to keep their shed staff and fitters employed and agreed to loan the engines for the weekend, but to have them returned for repairs and boiler-washing, etc, early the following week.

With the seasonal loss of work, the footplate staff was also put back in their grades and the junior passed cleaners were surplus to requirements. This meant that a job was available for the summer if they were prepared to go, on loan, to depots that were short of men. When things improved these men would be re-instated at their home depot without loss of seniority. If, on the other hand, they did not wish to go away on loan, then they would have to find other employment.

Many of these young men chose to go on loan, and some were allocated to Bath. They were found lodgings, some with railway families, others with people who lived near to the loco. They were mixed in with the Bath passed cleaners according to their seniority, and usually had a firing turn, at least, on Mondays, Fridays and Saturdays.

The engine Control at Derby were told early in the week the number of extra engines that were wanted for the week-end and these engines began to arrive from Wednesday night onwards. These were stabled in any space available until the Locomotive Department was filled to overflowing. The weekend working started with the up Pines being run in two parts on Friday. The relief part was for Sheffield and was worked by Bath men, who, with a Saltley pilotman from Birmingham, went to Sheffield. The engine was taken to Millhouses loco where the Bath men lodged. The return working was the down Pines (Sheffield portion) the next day.

The extra coaches that were required at Bournemouth and that could not be stored for use in the vicinity also had to be got there, so on Friday evenings there were these trains to run. On arrival at Bournemouth the train crews lodged at Branksome for an early return working to Bath on Saturday.

At certain times of the year pigeon specials were run from the Midlands and the North. These arrived late on Friday or early Saturday morning. Often these were for Pokesdown, Christchurch, Poole, and Bournemouth.

The Weymouth pigeon trains worked by Bath men were booked "short rest" and returned in the evening with their vans and baskets. There were also some that went onto the Southern at Templecombe. These trains were only required during the less busy times of the summer service. The men working these trains sometimes lodged at Branksome. The "Southern, via Templecombe" pigeon trains went forward with their own engines and men, so our engines and men either went to Templecombe loco or to some other job.

The early morning holiday train arrivals through Bath on a Saturday from the Midlands were manned either by a couple of Bath sets returning from Gloucester, or by Bristol, Derby or Saltley men. These Derby and Saltley men were sometimes booked to lodge at Bath, and to return to the Midlands about midday. There were several kindly older people who used to offer their spare beds to these men for a small reward. Of course arrangements would have been made for this service during the week, but I was occasionally called upon to conduct these men to these addresses when they did not know where to go. This was, may I say, in addition to my other duties as a bar boy.

There were only about three times that, owing to an acute shortage of engines, an S&D 7F 2-8-0 was allowed on any train other than a goods (except a breakdown train) before the 1939 war. This was when there were several pigeon specials to be dealt with and there were not enough engines. Mr Tom White, the chief foreman, would give permission for a 7F to work these trains provided that no fast running was made, and that the bearings were to be inspected whenever possible to ensure that no overheating was taking place.

At Branksome there were only five sets of men and all firemen were passed for driving, so by upgrading the passed cleaners extra sets could be made if required. Bath men who were lodging off the Friday empty stock trains, or wanting return working from a pigeon special would help out, but Templecombe loco depot would help also.

To get the number of sets that were required at Bath for the Saturday working, all goods trains were cancelled after the 10-30pm S&D goods on Friday on both the S&D and Midland routes, until the 7-50pm S&D goods on Saturday. There were neither men, engines nor track space to run any goods trains.

There were about 20 or so passed firemen at Bath, so with 40 or so passed cleaners at least 20 extra sets could be made up for use in the week-end working.

As there was no banking required at Radstock, crews from there were available for other work and were used at Bath. The firemen were often put on train jobs, while drivers were set to work on footplate shed duties, as they did not have the required road knowledge for train working, but they were quite happy to assist doing the various jobs of preparing, disposing and moving engines around the loco. This was the system of working into which I was plunged when my career as a locoman started. I was given two weeks' training to become a bar boy, then I had to take over on my own.

This was on the 6-00am turn, and the summer service was in full swing. Although I examined every engine tube-plate that arrived on the shed there were a couple of times when the call of "bar boy" was heard if fire-bars were missing or adrift when the fire was cleaned. On examination maybe new fire-bars were wanted. I would get them and replace them with the aid of a tool called a "pricker" (made from a fire-iron about eight feet long with a right-angled blade at the end, and used to manipulate fire-bars into position from the footplate). Often the men who were working the engine home on its return working towards the Midlands would be on the engine, and the clean fire would be next to the space where the new fire-bars were to go. When finished the fire would be spread over and made up for this return journey.

Although replacing fire-bars with a pricker in those days was a rare practice, it was a taste of future days when fire-bars would be lifted and replaced as a normal disposal practice.

It was about December 1937 when the bridges on the Mangotsfield Branch were strengthened and made ready to receive larger engines. When they came over the bridges they were subjected to various speed restrictions. The first to arrive, (I believe), was a Stanier Black; it came from Bristol to work a special towards the Midlands. Soon these engines were arriving on the down Pines and they were Nos.5268, 5271, 5274 and others. Whether they went back on the Derby Parcels, or were kept for the Pines the next day, I cannot recall.

It was difficult to clean the fire on these 5 Class engines using the long-handled clinker shovel to throw out the spent clinker owing to the high tender plate. Permission was given to lift fire-bars and drop the spent clinker into the ash-pan and then rake it out into the ash-pit. This practice was soon extended to all engines and it became the normal procedure.

One day in the early spring of 1938 a Stanier 5 Class No. 5288 arrived from Bristol to work a "Trial and Test Run" over the S&D. The next day a crew from the S&D goods link booked on and took the train to Bournemouth and back on this test run. This proved a success and soon there were six Stanier Blacks allocated to Bath. These were Nos. 5023, 5029, 5194, 5389, 5432 and 5440.

When these engines went into service the first to go over the S&D was 5440 on the 6-35pm passenger to Bournemouth on a Saturday night in place of the usual 2P. It was then to work the up Pines on the Monday, as was the normal working. The next 5 Class to go over the S&D was 5432 on the 10-20am passenger train from Bath to Bournemouth on the Monday.

Engine workings were soon changed, and a 5 Class was put on the 2-40am Mail to Bournemouth returning with Branksome men on the up Pines. The engine was then re-serviced at Bath before it worked the down Pines with the same Branksome men. This engine then returned to Bath on the 9-35pm goods with the Bath men who had lodged at Branksome from the 2.40am Mail. This engine was re-serviced again at Bath, and worked the 10-20am passenger to Bournemouth and back. It then went into the 2-40am Mail working again the next day. This was a two-day working, and so two Class 5 engines were employed.

With the arrival of the larger engines at Bath and over the S&D, they eased but did not end the engine shortages during the summer service. Trains from the Midlands with their 12-coach loads now arrived with one engine, and of course, when they returned they were now able to take their loads unassisted. Most of these trains had the larger engines. It was a different story on the S&D.

Although the six Stanier Class engines were fully employed, these were still not enough for the weekend workings. Some engines still had to be borrowed from other depots. Any spare engines that came onto the shed were still used if they could do a trip and arrive back in time for their booked return working.

Using larger engines over the S&D meant that assistance was now only required as far as Masbury as these engines could haul 12 coaches from there to Bournemouth. It was usual however to detach the assisting engine at Evercreech Junction and hold it there, after it was turned, to assist a train back to Bath that would be arriving and requiring assistance over the Mendips. This was a big saving of engine running and manpower.

During the spring of 1939 I was told to teach a new lad the bar boy's job, as I was getting towards 18 years of age. I told him about the job, the same as I had been told two years before. Then after the usual two weeks' training I was told to go in the cleaning gang the following week.

Starting cleaning was not what it seemed to be. Starting at 7-00am with the day gang, the chargeman cleaner detailed me to assist on some labouring work which required a left-handed person. This went on for several days, and as I was paid at the labouring rate of pay I had no complaints. When I was available, and a brick-arch had to be built, I would be sent to help. This meant getting the tools and bricks, then placing them all onto the footplate, while the fireclay was mixed and two side bricks cut to fit the firebox seam joint. I would then sit near to the fire-hole, and when all was ready, I would place all the supplies onto the fire-hole casting, in sequence, for building the brick-arch inside the firebox. I knew in what order the bricks would be wanted.

My seniority counted from the day that I had started in the Locomotive Department; this made me senior to a lot of passed cleaners in the gang. This meant that I was sent on labouring duties to load ashes, unload sand, load and unload supplies, as required. These were classed as senior jobs and were paid at labouring rates of pay. Most of the passed cleaners were on the same rate of pay while cleaning, as with myself, so this made little difference. This work was instead of   cleaning engines which was the job left when all these better paid jobs had been taken. This fact does not seem to be important in modern times, but in 1939 to be paid a higher wage, if only a few shillings a week, meant that a few extras could be afforded that otherwise would be denied.

On reaching the age of 18 years, I asked if I might try to pass the examination required to become a passed cleaner or should I say a spare fireman. After the Superintendent had finished his other business I was sent for and after his examination he was satified that I was able to be used for firing duties. After a medical examination by the doctor I was told to read the footplate staff requirement sheets daily to see if I was required for firing duties.

Friday came and I was booked out for Saturday on an express assisting job over the S&D section. I arrived in good time and booked on. We then prepared No.632 and coupled up to a 4F. My driver was a passed fireman whom I had often helped, when he was on a relief turn and disposing an engine. He knew that this was my first trip as a fireman so he gave me every assistance, with any bits of advice that he could. We did the job satisfactorily and returned to Bath tender first, where the engine was put in order for another job. We did a couple more jobs on the shed to make up our day's work before going home. My spare firing days had now begun.

Firing Days
to Flying Days

Various jobs came my way as I took my position, in seniority, in the cleaning gang. Several times a week I was booked out firing and went to such places as Bournemouth, Weymouth, Templecombe and Evercreech, also on loan to Radstock. All these jobs were on both passenger and goods trains.

Being in the passed cleaners gang meant that one gang started at 7-00am; the other gang was put on a night shift to cover any spare firing that might occur during the 24-hour day. Booking on at 6-00pm, the night gang would assemble in the drivers' lobby and await the foreman's orders.

Should a request be made to run a 7-15pm special goods then the senior man would be told to go on the 7-50pm goods with the driver. The next man was told to go on the special running at 7-15pm with the passed fireman, originally the passed fireman on the 7-50pm, as the driver. The next man would be told to go to Radstock as passenger on the 6-35pm, to be the fireman on the banker and join up with a Radstock man as the driver to assist the 7.15pm up the bank to Masbury. I went to Radstock on this job one night and returned with the 10-20pm passenger arrival to Bath. Later that week it was decided to run the 7-15pm special goods again, but this time I was the oldest passed cleaner so I went on the 7-50pm goods to Evercreech Junction on 13805 7F 2-8-0. This was my first trip on one of these engines. I was amazed at the working, and stopping power, of this class of engine. My next turn was a job disposing and preparing engines.

Within a few trips I found myself at Bournemouth on a Saturday special. When passing Broadstone I saw a derailed Southern Schools Class engine No.933 *King's Canterbury*. This was the first derailment that I had seen.

When we arrived on Branksome shed I was amazed to find so many engines on so small a shed. Engines were everywhere, not only S&D ones, but Southern ones as well. These had called in for reservicing after their trip from Waterloo, and were being got ready for their return trip. The messroom was filled with men, but a good supply of hot drinking water was on hand to make the tea. After putting our engine right we had a wash, and had our meal break sat on the engine. Our engine from Bath had been a 4F 0-6-0, and our assisting engine, a 2P 4-4-0, had come through to Bournemouth with us; we both turned on the turntable and re-coupled in readiness for the return trip. The load was to be 12 coaches back to Bath, the same as it had been from Bath.

The larger engines, being too long for the turntable, had to turn on the triangle which was on the main-line junction near to the loco. Some of the other trains had the same power arrangements as ourselves.

The building of Class 5 engines was still not completed. Those that had been built were put on regular jobs, replacing the overloaded, and lower-powered older types. This left the holiday trains, excursions, pigeon, and other extra trains to get what engines they could from any source available. Normally the larger engines that could be "borrowed" for S&D work were either a 2-6-0 Crab or a 5 Class 4-6-0. This was when a spare trip could be done while waiting for the return to the Midlands from Bath.

I never saw a 5XP on the S&D, although at one time No.5612 *Jamaica* was allocated to Bath to work the Pines over the Midland section.

I recall that every year, for several years pre-war, on a particular Saturday morning four or five special trains, each with a 14-coach load and reserved for the Leicester Co-op staff, came through Bath from Leicester to Bournemouth for their annual holidays. These trains returned on the following Saturday. There were always two 4F 0-6-0 engines put on each of these trains at Bath for their journey over the S&D section.

One day the call boy advised me that I was required for the 10-20pm Derby Parcels that night. This train started as the 8-25pm from Templecombe, and was called the Perishables. Then from Bath it went to Derby as the Rabbits. From Birmingham it was known as the Derby Parcels.

I had never had a firing turn over the Midland route, and this was to be my 23rd firing turn, so I arrived at work in plenty of time for the job.   Although the engine, No.635, a 2P 4-4-0, had been prepared, I had a good look around to make sure that all was in order for when the driver arrived. When he did arrive he asked me "who is my fireman?" and when I told him that I had been called upon to do the job he started to complain of how unfairly he had been treated to be given such a young lad to do this job. Never once did he consider that it would be me that had to get the steam for his requirements for the 193 miles that lay before us. Neither did he give a thought that I had never been north of Mangotsfield before.

We went out onto the train and before long we set off on our journey. Onward we went until the lights of a city came into view. "Good, Birmingham" I thought, but alas this was only Gloucester. We stopped and took water and extra vans were put onto the rear of the train while we were doing this. The first time that my driver spoke to me since we had left Bath was when he shouted "Water" and we were to refill the tender tank with water when we stopped at Gloucester.

Away we went again now with a full load until we stopped at Bromsgrove for four bankers to assist us up the Lickey Incline with our load of about 25 vans. The next time that my driver spoke to me was when we passed Northfield, near Kings Norton, when he shouted "Damper" which I then closed. Soon after, he closed the regulator and we coasted into Birmingham New Street. We were uncoupled on arrival at the station, then we turned the engine around, took water and I got the coal forward for my use on the return journey. Then when I had put the fire in order, I was able to wash my hands and have my sandwiches.

Soon we went out onto the return train, which was a parcels train from Leicester. We had to shunt this train which was rather a complicated affair. It was impossible to see the shunter, as we were in a tunnel and were enveloped in steam. The signalman could not see the shunter either, so after going forewards the shunter applied the brake to stop us when we were over the points. He then sounded a horn (similar to a hunting horn) using a code. The signalman, knowing the code, altered the points to which track was required. The shunter, then seeing that this was done, released the brake and the driver would then set back to complete the move. When all was in order we set off towards Bath calling at Cheltenham, where we took water, then to Gloucester where we attached several Southern vans, empties from previous rabbit traffic. When we arrived at Bath we took the engine to the shed where someone else disposed of it. I went home very tired but pleased to have had another successful trip.

There seemed to be a war approaching and all the goods trains from the S&D were made up to full banker loads from Evercreech Junction to Bath by adding extra empty wagons if there was the space. These wagons were made into special trains of vans, private owner coal wagons, or railway-owned open wagons on arrival at Bath. These were sent towards the Midlands and to wherever they were wanted in train loads of 50 wagons. These trains left Bath at 12-25am, 4-00am, and 10-45am. The train crews were booked to Birmingham where they were to lodge at Saltley Barracks. As well as coal trains on the return trips, there were also train-loads of barbed wire from the Midlands that were to go over the S&D in loads of 57 wagons.

These specials over the S&D, when required, were run in the usual times of 5-00am, 2-00pm, or 7-15pm. The Midland and S&D special goods were crewed by passed firemen and passed cleaners. I was in the position where I was eligible for these jobs and was booked on them many times. For a long while I was booked to work a special goods to Birmingham and lodge, have 9 hours' rest at Saltley, then work a return trip to Bath, have 12 hours' rest, then back to Birmingham again.

These jobs seemed to be straightforward enough, getting an engine ready at Bath and going to Birmingham, but after getting to Barnt Green the working generally was put onto the goods line, then at Halesowen onto "Permissive Block" and to be lined up head to tail with the train in front until Kings Norton was reached.

As many of the trains were waiting to go beyond Birmingham and there was no relief for the crews available, this would cause hours of delay until relief men could be found and the trains could proceed to Landor Street for relief. The same thing would often happen at the same places in the reverse direction. The extra goods trains would be lined up between Kings Norton and Barnt Green, but the problem here was the shortage of track space and time to allow them to proceed between the normal services.

On being relieved at Landor Street we would walk to Saltley loco, book off, and get a lodge ticket allowing us to use the Barracks. This was a Victorian building that looked more like a jail than anything else. On entering the building, in the hall was the janitor's desk and the information board where all the men, their depots, and the time that they were to be called was marked against the room numbers which they were allocated.

To the right of the hall was a corridor where on the left was the kitchen containing a large gas stove with about a dozen rings. There were also pots and pans of all descriptions, as well as a great many plates and teapots. The messroom was on the right of the corridor which had several tables and chairs.

Nothing except food, plates, cups, and cutlery was allowed to be placed on the tables. All bags, boxes and anything else was to be placed on the floor. Onward through the messroom was the reading room, where men could sit, read their own newspapers, or an old magazine long out of date, to wait for a bed to be booked to them. When a room was allocated it was marked on the board, but no one informed you.

The bedrooms were upstairs. On the left on the first floor was "A" dormitory, a large room with eight cubicles each side of a central aisle. On the right was "B" dormitory, exactly the same. Between both dormitories were rooms 17A & 18A. These were two rooms that were for light sleepers as they were complete rooms in themselves. The other rooms were separated off with seven-foot high wooden walls.

Each room had a bed with a straw mattress (which seemed never to have been turned). When you got into bed it was impossible to fall out, as it was like sleeping in a gutter. These beds were usually referred to by the locomen as "smokeplates" (a fire-hole deflector plate). There was a wooden chair that was used to put your clothes on, but the back was put under the doorknob to keep the door secure, as their was no lock, while the occupant was asleep. There was also a small chamber pot.

The window was nailed shut, but the view outside was of gas supply mains pipes in their storage yard. Inside the dormitory, the noise was sometimes very disturbing. Often there was snoring, or flatulence, and even sleep-talking. During these times I was able to sleep anywhere, but I was always ready to get up when the janitor knocked on the door and said "Bath men so and so time" with my reply of "thank-you". We then got up, had a wash and a meal, which we had to provide ourselves and had carried from home, then off to Saltley loco to book on and find out what our return job would be. The guard would be included throughout in the crew at the Barracks.

With more men lodging at Saltley it was decided to build another wing onto the Barracks in the form of a series of single rooms. Although there were already 68 beds in use these were not enough for the requirements. Meanwhile the overflow was put into pre-war camping coaches that were in the carriage sheds at Lawley Street, or into another hostel at Aston. The new wing, when opened, was excellent, very quiet and with interior sprung mattresses, etc. It was good to have a comfortable rest for a change.

When I was on a lodging job, I used to take my food in a cloth shopping bag. There were no canteens available so I had to carry all supplies with me. I used to carry a two-pound loaf of bread, a tub of margarine, a jar of tea and one of condensed milk, a tin of beans, an egg, bacon or sausages, whenever they were available, and anything else that would help to fill me up. If we could visit the market at Birmingham or a kindly shopkeeper, a pork pie or pasty would be welcome. I also knew all the chip shops between Bath and Birmingham. Extra rations of tea, sugar and hard tack biscuits were supplied at Bath loco but these had to be paid for and the book signed for double-home men. If my food ran out on a trip then none was available until I reached home. During the many hours that we spent in sidings, one of us would be able to get some sort of rest in the cab, but this was certainly not comfortable.

Sometimes a good run could be had and we would get home in a few hours. I recall one bad trip, however, when we booked on one Friday evening at 8.30pm and arrived at Bath 36 hours later at 8.30am on Sunday morning. Booking on at Saltley we prepared a 4F 0-6-0, then went to Washwood Heath and backed on to a coal train for Bath. Arriving at Kings Norton we were put into the queue of waiting goods trains. It seemed that every siding and space between there and Cheltenham was occupied. The cause of this delay was that there was the usual bottleneck of trains between Cheltenham and Gloucester as this was only a two-track section which the GWR shared with the LMS. The former always wanted to use this track for all their extra freight trains going from Birmingham to South Wales, Swindon and Gloucester, which were in addition to all our LMS trains. With the passenger service given priority, our humble coal train was the last consideration. We eventually reached Gloucester late on Saturday night, having advised the Control that we required coal; I had cleaned the fire en route. After we left Gloucester we again went into every siding as the trains in front of us were waiting to get into Westerleigh sidings and we did not reach Bath till the next morning. It would have been useless to have asked for relief, as there was none available.

For this particular week's work I was paid for 119 hours allowing for overtime. The week's pay account started at the first time of booking on duty after 12.01am on Sunday. Six turns of eight hours per day formed the normal week's work, when working between 6.00am and 10.00pm; working between 10.00pm and 6.00am was paid as time and a quarter, as was overtime; Sunday working paid time and three-quarters and booking on duty on a Sunday counted as an extra turn outside the normal working week.

I was a single man at the time, but I had told my mother not to worry about when I got home, because if anything was amiss owing to air raids or mishap then the railway company would soon let her know what had happened.

One evening we booked on at Saltley and were given our orders, with about 20 other crews, to travel in some brake vans hauled by an engine and relieve some trains that were between Kings Norton and Bromsgrove. Many were "on the block" (lined up behind each other, with the engine of the second train against the guard's van of the first train) on the goods road.

At each brake van and engine we stopped and the men concerned changed over. Our train was in this queue. After a couple of moves forward my driver told me to enquire from the signalman at Northfield what our chances were. His reply was that when we relieved our train it had been about tenth in the queue, and it was hopeless for some while. After about eight hours we got towards the front of the queue when we were ourselves relieved. Along with all the other relieved crews we went to Bromsgrove where an express was stopped and we all travelled home.

When the war started I had been doing all sorts of trips; some were on the S&D on both passenger and goods trains, troop trains, and all sorts of military equipment trains. Mainly I was either lodging at Birmingham, taking empty wagons from Bath and a train of loaded goods wagons or a train of coal back, or I was going to Bournemouth on the 2-40am Mail and lodging there.

One night we booked on at Saltley and were told to relieve engine 40XX, a 4F 0-6-0 at Washwood Heath West End on a train for Bristol. There was an air raid on, but we wanted to get home. To foil air attacks, pots of creosote were used to give off fumes which obscured the ground from above. These fumes irritated the eyes and breathing, and along with the fumes given off from Saltley Gas Works it was very unpleasant. Our train stood outside the signalbox; all was dark and quiet. It was a Class A (a non-vacuum through freight). No head-lamps were lit. We tapped on the cab-side and told the men that we were to relieve them. The men got off and said that there were 39 wagons on, all for Bristol and hurried away. Their guard soon went by so we knew that our guard was aboard the train. What puzzled me was what type of train we had, but this was not for long. My driver told me to have a look. It was a train of barrage balloon gas on trailers. I told my driver as the raid was still on. He told me to inform the signalman what was outside of his box. Everyone was then alerted and soon we were on our way out of Birmingham to

Bristol. We put the train into the sidings at Fishponds (Bristol) and took the engine to Bath.

All goods trains were loaded either to a full load or a full length during these times. One night we had a 3F 0-6-0 on the 9-15pm Bath to Birmingham goods. We called at Westerleigh and Gloucester. Although we were fully laden we did very well, but when we were about a mile from Bromsgrove the weight of the train pulled us to a stand. The steam pressure was 15 lbs below full pressure, but when this was regained we were able to pull the train into the station. It was slightly uphill at this point.

Working over the Lickey Incline in either direction meant special workings. In the up direction, all trains, when passing Stoke Works, had to sound one "pop" on the whistle for every banker it required, according to the load. If four "pops" were sounded then four bankers were sent out to assist when the train stopped at Bromsgrove.

The large 0-10-0 tender engine *Big Bertha* counted as two 0-6-0 tank 3F bankers. The engines were placed at the rear, but were not coupled up to the train, or to themselves. After exchanging whistle codes the train went up the bank, but on nearing the top of the incline first one banker would drop away, then another and so forth, and the train went on its way unhindered and the bankers returned from Blackwell to Bromsgrove.

On the down direction the passenger, parcels, and vacuum-fitted goods train went down the bank with a speed limit of 60mph.

The goods and freight trains, being loose coupled and without a continuous brake, had to stop at the summit and have the brakes of the wagons applied. The practice was that as the train slowly passed the brakesman and the guard of the train, they would in sequence drop the first brake handle out of its rack so as to rub the wheel, pin down the next brake onto the wheel, then miss the next wagon brake, and so forth until the driver felt that sufficient brakes were applied for him to control the descent of the train on the two miles of 1/37 downward gradient. He would then sound the whistle and no more brakes would be applied.

One evening we booked on at Saltley after lodging and went to Washwood Heath on a Class 3F where we coupled onto a train of coal for Bath. Arriving at the top of Bromsgrove bank we were drawing the train over the top and the brakesman and guard were beginning to put the brakes down when the engine lurched forwards. As my driver closed the regulator and applied the brake, the rear of the train came into us and pushed us with considerable force down the bank. Away we went with no hope of stopping. Of course the engine's brakes, although fully on, were useless for the weight of the train and not enough brakes had been applied on the wagons by the brakesman. With the whistle blowing to warn everyone of our plight, the signalman at Bromsgrove North, seeing our position, set the points to let us have a free run on the main line. Eventually we came to a stand nearing Stoke Works, far beyond where we should have stopped. We were pulled back to Bromsgrove where it was found that the brake gear on the guards van had broken and was useless. The van was changed and our engine examined. When the guard had been brought back from Blackwell to rejoin the train, we set off once more on our journey.

On 10th May 1940, I was booked to go to Leeds on that portion of the Pines. It was the 12-08pm from Bath. We prepared 5194 and with 12 coaches on we set off and arrived at 6-26pm. During the journey I noticed that many of the military personnel were questioned by the Military Police and redirected to go to another destination. On taking the engine to Holbeck shed it was at once booked up to work the Glasgow Parcels. We lodged at the Barracks, which was next to the coal hopper. The lodge was very clean, but no frying pans were supplied. Eggs and bacon, etc, would be cooked in a baking tin in the oven. Before going upstairs to the bedroom, footwear had to be removed. The room that we were allocated had two single beds in it. During the evening we had a walk and found ourselves in *The White Swan*. There was a Social Evening upstairs in the clubroom, we were invited, and a very pleasant time was had by all.

The next day when we reported for work we were told that our train had been cancelled and we had to travel home as passengers. The war in France had escalated and the armies were on the move. When we arrived home we were asked about 5194 and we told the foreman what had happened. When the engine was traced it was reported to be running around on a passenger train between Perth and Inverness. Eventually it arrived home five days later.

Some nights later I was booked up on the 9-15pm goods to Birmingham and lodge. This train was cancelled, however, owing to troops being evacuated from Dunkirk.

From the S&D came two empty stock trains, one with 11 empty coaches on, and the other with 10. Both trains were joined together with our Class 5 engine. An assisting engine, a 2P 4-4-0, 500 Class, came onto the front, and we set off northwards with these 21 coaches. Unfortunately the fire-hole doors on this 2P jammed open as soon as we left Bath and it was decided to detach this engine at Gloucester, and as there was no other engine available we were to go on with this train on our own. My driver was relieved at Landor Street, while I had to go on to Walsall, where a Class 8F took the train forward, while we returned to Saltley. I rejoined my driver at the Barracks where we lodged. Later that day we returned to Bath with a coal train.

On one trip home from Saltley I was kept busy throwing pieces of slate over the side from our coal supply. Someone, when loading the coal hopper, had tipped in a wagon-load of slates that was intended for use in repairing the shed roof and had become mixed with the coal wagons. These slates went into the hopper as if they had been coal.

One Saturday night on 20th January 1940, I was on 3826 and going to Birmingham on a double-home job. We had the usual rake of empties and the night was very cold. The night turned out to be the coldest for 50 years. When we emerged from Wickwar Tunnel the steam pressure gauge, instead of registering 175 lbs, went back to 120 lbs and remained there. It had frozen.

We carried on, but with no gauge to refer to it was a very difficult situation. When we got near to Bromsgrove the engine blew off steam. This was the first time since the freeze up. While going along on our journey my driver took off his boot and placed his foot near to the firehole but, although his sock was scorching he could feel nothing as his foot was very cold. When we arrived at Bromsgrove there was a set of men trying to unfreeze the water column bag. After a struggle they did manage it. We were then able to take water and continue on to Landor Street where we had relief with the gauge still frozen. As we walked to Saltley loco the train passed us but the wagons were squealing as the axle-boxes were still frozen.

The return working of the 9-15pm Bath to Birmingham goods was to sign on, go to Exchange sidings and relieve Saltley men, and work the 1-45am to Bath. One night the train was diverted via Redditch. We were supplied with a pilotman, and my driver decided to ride in the guards van. This of course gave more room on the footplate, as there were several tablet exchanges to be made, and the room was wanted to work from either side. I had never been over this route before, and as it was a dark and moonless night I saw nothing of where we were going either. Having exchanged tokens by hand before on several jobs on the S&D, when no catcher was available, I was not at a loss of how to do this; the only information needed was on which side to make the exchange.

It was a good experience for me, but not so pleasant for my mate who was in the brake van. His story was that the wheels of the van had flats, which made the ride very rough, and it was also a "rocker" (overdue for an overhaul and with a lot of side play). The guard, after starting, wedged himself in and dared not move while the train was moving. There was no need to work the hand brake as it was a vacuum-fitted train. My mate was tossed from one side of the van to the other and he admitted that at one point he had tried to sit on the wheel of the hand brake but he was unable to hang on. I don't think he ever volunteered to ride in a brake van again.

One night I was booked on the Avonmouth goods. While getting the return train ready there was an air raid alert. Everyone went to the shelter as there was activity nearby. Some while later it became quiet so we went back to our train. We heard no other sound except that from our engine, but saw in the sky a burst of flame from something that had caught fire and was floating down to earth. This happened several times.

We left Avonmouth not knowing what it was. Afterwards we were told that these fireballs had been barrage balloons catching fire in an electrical storm.

On a goods train it was a work of art to get through Clifton Down Tunnel. The difficult part was to keep the train moving and not get stopped at the Starter signal at Sea Mills. Usually a local passenger to Bristol passed by on the main line as we were waiting on the goods line at the starting signal. Going out onto the main line when the passenger train was clear, and going slowly, this allowed the passenger to call at Shirehampton and Sea Mills, and to arrive at Clifton Down station so that we could get the Sea Mills Distant signal in the clear position.

Sea Mills signalbox was switched out at night so the signals were controlled by Clifton Down. If these signals were clear then the goods could have a clear run to Clifton Down and get up speed to go through the tunnel. This tunnel was a bit of a devil, and with a heavy train, full power was needed. If the engine blew off steam then the wheels would be sure to slip, and momentum would be lost before regaining grip again. This, along with the rails being wet in places, could result in a train crawling out of the tunnel very slowly. Although the tunnel was, at that time, double line, the smoke from the engines passing through made it very foggy, and it was often impossible to know when you were about to emerge from the tunnel. As the gradient was steep and the trains were going slow, a little warning device was installed to aid drivers so as to be able to stop at the signal placed about 200 yards from the mouth of the tunnel. This was in the form of a "clapper" which was operated by the train wheels. When this sounded, by looking out of the cab at a height of about 4 feet, one could see the Distant signal light. To hear the clap, clap, of the device was a great help to all footplate crews.

As the months passed I gradually progressed towards becoming a senior passed cleaner, and I was booked on regular jobs instead of specials. The jobs, on the morning shift would often be the 12-16am Bath banker, or the 2-40am Mail, or the 3-30am, all S&D turns. The afternoon jobs could be the 12-45pm S&D goods, or a local Midland goods turn.

During this period I had to register for military service and, after some tests and examinations, I was selected to go into the RAF for training to become a pilot. When my call-up papers arrived, I was on the 2-40am Mail, lodging, for the week's work.

I had to report to Air Crew Receiving Centre for training. After joining I had to sit various grading examinations and was put into a flight of 50 trainee pilots, and posted to an Initial Training Wing where we had our ground training. Then we were posted to a Flying School. Passing this stage we went to other flying schools in Canada. After a long while I was taken off flying duties for medical reasons and it was decided that I should return home to England, and be discharged and return to my previous employment.

My Second Spell
on the S&D

Returning to the railway at Bath in 1942, I was told that during my absence there were juniors who had been upgraded and made firemen, but there was a vacancy and that I would take my place on the next list to become a registered fireman.

Several things had changed since I had left. The 5 Class and the 2P 4-4-0 engines, except for about two, had been transferred and replaced by Southern 4-4-0 engines, Nos.398-404. It was on these engines that I would have to work when I took my rostered position in the S&D passenger link on the second week back on the job, where there was a vacancy. This turned out to be my rightful job and I became a registered fireman within a few weeks.

Before this first trip I had a quick look around these engines. I had seen, but had never taken any notice of them before, so I had to find out how the injectors worked, the shape of the fire they liked, and other such details. I went with my driver onto the engine and after relieving the preparing crew we set off on our journey, a passenger train to Templecombe.

The S&D passenger link was the senior link for drivers but, at that time, the junior link for firemen. All the jobs were train work but the only route was between Bath and Templecombe. The earliest job was on duty at 1-10am to prepare our engine, and get the mail van from the station, then couple to and assist the 2-40am Mail to Evercreech Junction.

If this train was a bank load, then the Bath banker would bank out of Bath but the coupled engine would become the banker from Radstock and remain on the rear until Evercreech Junction where it would detach and work the 5-35am goods to Templecombe Lower. Then after turning the loco it would go onto the 7-15am passenger coaches in the lower sidings, and pull both Bournemouth and Bath portions out of the sidings, where the engine for the Bournemouth portion would back onto the rear, and both portions would go to the station. Both portions would remain coupled until stopping at Templecombe Junction after leaving the station, where they would part, going their separate ways.

Our train to Bath would stop at all stations, and was due at Bath at 8-43am. This was a school children and office workers service. On this job the engine was either an LMS 2P 4-4-0 or an SR 4-4-0 type engine.

The 6-55am and the 8-30am passenger trains were worked with a 4F 0-6-0 type. Either could have the parcels vans from the Midlands attached, depending on the arrival time of the parcels train. The 8-30am engine remained at Templecombe and worked the 8-25pm Perishables back to Bath at night. These two jobs were difficult for a fireman during the steam heating period, as most 4F Class locos on the S&D were right-hand drive, and all the stations were on the left-hand side. This meant that the fireman had to be disengaged at every station so as to get the guard's signal to depart. With the steam heating pipes leaking it was a full-time job for the fireman at every station. If the parcels vans had been put onto the rear of the train, as they were not needed en route, the train would have been made more compact, the passengers would have received more benefit from the heating, and the guard would have been nearer to the train crew and more easily seen.

The other day job was the 10-20am semi-fast to Temple-combe. At one time, after relief at Templecombe, there was a long wait before we relieved our return working, so we had to take to an SR tank engine, one of Nos.1-5, and go to Stalbridge with a couple of wagons to shunt the goods yard. The two afternoon jobs were the 2-53pm and the 4-25pm from which we returned with the Perishables and the Last Up passenger.

I would point out that at this stage of the war the coal supplies were getting short, and it was a case that any sort of fuel was tipped onto tenders, and the firemen had to do their best with it. Briquettes and all sorts of coal and coke were supplied. These "bricks" came in all shapes and sizes. The large ones of about 10 inches cube, if tipped onto an SR 4-4-0 tender and not broken up, were a disaster if they got wedged in the coal shovelling hole on the tender. These large bricks would have to be got out separately and broken, and it took some time before normal firing work could be resumed. If they had been broken before tipping onto the tender then this could have been avoided, though sometimes this did happen.

Sometimes there was a mixture of bricks and household coal. This was a poor mixture, as the Welsh bricks did not require as much secondary air to burn satisfactorily as the northern coal, but whichever way it was decided to burn this mixture good results could not be achieved.

At one loco shed that we called at to get coal, I was surprised to see a good grade of northern coal being tipped onto our tender. Being curious I looked at the wagon label and saw, to my amazement, that the wagon should have been for a local coal merchant. I had a word with the railway coalman who did not know that anything was wrong. He removed the labels and replaced them on another wagon of northern coal of the same weight content which was for the Locomotive Department. To my knowledge no-one else had spotted the mistake, and everything passed off without further ado.

One evening, on the Last Up passenger from Templecombe to Bath, we were stopped at Cole station by signals. I was sent to the signalbox to ask "why the delay?" and was told that an aircraft had struck the chimney of a level crossing keeper's house and some of the bricks had fallen onto the track. When this mess had been removed we could then be allowed to proceed. Some sailors asked me what the trouble was, so I told them. In good humour, they told some airmen that it was a good job that they were not trusted with a battleship.

My time in this link eventually came to an end and I was put into the Midland passenger link. There were eight turns in this link, four of ordinary 0-4-4 tank engine jobs between Bath and Bristol (St Philip's), and two turns of "push-and-pull" 0-4-4 tank engine workings. The other two jobs were the Midland Pines and the Derby Parcels.

The push-and-pull job was to push four special coaches from Bath to Bristol on a local service, then pull the train to Wickwar with workers for the nearby factories; then take empty coaches back to Bristol carriage sidings; after that, into Barrow Road loco and reservice the engine; then work a two-set to Bath. On relief at Bath, the afternoon set would do the same job, only in reverse order except for the reservicing of the engine.

What was special about push-pull working was that while pushing the train, the driver would be in his compartment in the leading coach at the other end of the train, and would have his brake apparatus and a valve that would shut off regulator steam to the engine cylinders. Only the fireman was aboard the engine at the other end of the train. The usual engine for this job was 1348, an 0-4-4 1P tank. The other engines for this local service were Nos.1251, 1334 and 1408.

The coaches on the normal trains were either a Southern four-coach set, or a Midland two-coach set. While I was in this link, the war ended and things began to return very slowly to normal.

It was decided to restart the Mutual Improvement Class. This was a meeting where footplate staff would get together and discuss all aspects of their job including the working of engines, rules and regulations, and anything else of interest. I went along to this meeting and, to my surprise, was chosen as the Chairman and Instructor of the class. Every Sunday morning during the winter months we met and had a discussion in our endeavour to gain a better knowledge of the job. A subject was selected for the following Sunday morning and I as the Instructor, would prepare and give a lesson on this subject. One Sunday it might be on a part of the Rules and Regulations, and the next week, maybe, on how the valves and pistons on the Stevenson Link Motion operated. This went on throughout the season. Everyone joined in and asked questions or were questioned themselves about the subject. We had many a pleasant meeting discussing all these things.

One of the other turns in this link was the Midland Pines from Bath to Gloucester and back. We used to sign on duty and prepare the engine, work the train to Gloucester and then be relieved. After a meal break, we would relieve and work the down Pines back to Bath. After getting to the shed we disposed the engine and then maybe we would service another engine before booking off duty.

Of the six Stanier 5 Class that were originally shedded at Bath, four had been transferred while I was in the RAF and now the other two, 5029 and 5440, were to go. It was also decided to cancel the 2-40am Mail couple turn, and to put a 4F 0-6-0 on the 2-40am Mail with Bath Midland goods link men to go as far as Templecombe. There they were relieved by Templecombe men, who worked the train to Bournemouth and the up Pines back as far as Wincanton. The Bath men on being relieved at Templecombe would then prepare and work the 7-15am passenger to Bath, usually with No.4417, an 0-6-0.

The Bath men on the Midland Pines turn were now booked to travel to Wincanton on the 8-30am passenger and relieve these Templecombe men who worked the up Pines with the same engine that they had relieved the Bath men on with the 2.40am Mail. This engine, an 0-6-0 4F, was all right for the eight-coach load now allocated to the Pines workings.

One of the engines most frequently used on this turn was No.4422. This particular engine was in good condition, it steamed well, and above all it was one of the strongest engines at the depot, and was the "master" when pulling the load of 240 tons over the Mendip banks.

On the Midland section of the Pines we had an assortment of engines; they came in all shapes and sizes. We never knew what was booked until we saw the engine allocation board at the shed, or when it came into sight when we were to relieve the men at Gloucester. It could be a Stanier 5, a 5XP, a Compound, a 2-6-0 Crab or maybe a Baby Scot (Patriot). I have had a 3P 4-4-0 of the 715 Class several times on the Midland Pines.

One day, we were about to relieve Saltley men on the down Pines at Gloucester. From around the bend and about to enter the station I saw the train coming, but there was a strange class of engine hauling it. It was a Royal Scot 6122 *Royal Ulster Rifleman*. We relieved the crew and went on to Bath. I had never been on one of these engines before, neither had my driver. I must say that I thought it to be a very good engine. This was one of the first of its class to arrive at Bath. Obviously this engine was out of course and it soon went back to the Midlands, probably on the Derby Parcels.

Compounds were the most common type on the Midland side. It was always a rough trip if No.1000 or 1001 were on the job; they were very shy for steam. The better ones were 917 and 935 (Bournville engines).

The other turn in the link was the Derby Parcels. The workings were similar to what I was called upon to do just after I first started firing. The engine was still prepared for us, but was off the down Pines, a larger and stronger type; also the engine was taken to the station, and the shunting done for us. We still went to Birmingham, but we were relieved there, and then in turn relieved a parcels train from Leicester. Instead of returning via Dunhamstead, we were routed via the Redditch Branch. We still stopped at Cheltenham and Gloucester, but seldom picked up any vans at Gloucester as the rabbit traffic was no longer available.

One night on the Derby Parcels we had a Baby Scot No.5538 *Giggleswick*. From the start the exhaust injector would not work. Then when we passed Mangotsfield the live steam injector kept giving trouble. My driver said that we should ask for another engine from Gloucester. On passing Charfield we "popped" the whistle and shone our lamp, indicating our requirements to the signalman and was acknowledged by him. On arrival at Gloucester we changed engines and were given a 4F 0-6-0 which had just been prepared. For fuel it had coke and briquette dust. The firebox was filled with this mixture, but I could see no flames, although I could hear the sound of the coke crackling. On starting away with a full load the engine wheels slipped and the fire settled about four inches. When the engine's safety valves lifted the engine boiler primed, but if the pressure fell from the full pressure of 175 lbs to below 160 lbs the brakes started to apply. How long we took to get to Birmingham I do not know, as I had a full-time job looking at the steam gauge and shovelling this mixture of fuel into the firebox in my endeavour to keep the steam pressure and water level within limits. We told the Saltley men of our ordeal, but they decided to take the train on to Derby. We had a meal break and then relieved the Leicester to Bath Parcels.

While my driver did the shunting I often had to get the coal forward to be ready for our return journey. We also had to take water as the next convenient place was not until we reached Cheltenham.

One night I was about to take the single-line tablet at Barnt Green, where we started our diversion from the main line to go via Redditch and Evesham. I saw the signalman holding up the single-line token pouch, but when we got there he was returning to his box. I shouted for my driver to stop as I did not have the tablet. Going back to the signalbox I asked where the tablet was, but the signalman said that he had given it to me. We found he had hung the pouch on the mechanical lubricator handle of our 5 Class. There were eight tablet-changing signalboxes for the several single-line sections between Barnt Green and Evesham.

At one place, Redditch South, there was a woman working the signalbox, and I had to take a single-line token pouch from her. Here it was necessary to have the regulator open at the point where I had to take the tablet. This was owing to a bad single-line tunnel just in advance. Engines, at that time, had steam blowing from all joints when the regulator was open, but this lady would stand there, enveloped in steam, with the tablet held high. Many times I have not seen her until I was about four feet away, but I never failed to get the tablet. I never did speak to her, except to shout out "right" when I got the tablet. This was an early morning trip, and I only went over this route twice in daylight. Neither did I go over this route in the up direction.

One morning when I was working this turn during the war, it was getting towards dawn when we saw masses of aircraft, many towing gliders, but all going towards the South. No-one knew what it was, but we could tell that there was something big taking place. When we got to Bath we were told that D-Day had begun.

While I was in this link, the 4800 series of Class 5s were built. Some had grease nipple big ends; these were 4813, 4814, and 4815. How long this modification lasted I do not know. I was also in the link when the 73000 Class 5 British Standard, came out. The first of this class often worked the Pines and Parcels. All were allocated to 17A shed (Derby). We had most of these first twelve on the Pines and Parcels turns.

Regarding engine failures, while I was in this link I recall that one night on the up trip we arrived at Gloucester with a knocking from the gearing. On examination we found that the oilcap feeding a small end was missing and the metal had fused in the bush. This was on a 3P 4-4-0 715 Class. Engines were changed and we went forward with a 0-6-0 4F Class.

Another night we relieved the Leicester Parcels at Birmingham, again on a 3P 4-4-0, No.715, but on arrival we were told by the men that the right driving axlebox was hot. Believe me it *was* hot; it was glowing with heat. My driver told me to find the Locomotive Department Supervisor which I did. He arrived in a short while and after a few words he said to my mate "aren't you going to take her then, driver?" Knowing my driver I quickly got onto the engine and out of the way because I knew that with a remark like this, although my driver was a kindly man, if he was upset and knew that he was in the right, he would stand no messing, and a few strong words would be flowing. I do not think that he stopped swearing for about 10 minutes. The Supervisor got the message and departed, saying that he had better find something else. A 2P 4-4-0, No.509 or 511, was sent out and when we had changed over we went forward with this engine.

There were two occasions when there was a crash of ironwork onto the footplate. This was when the firehole door framework fell apart. This was the dropdoor type, and the lot just came adrift. Both times were when we were on our way home from Birmingham on the Parcels. We did not stop as I managed to secure the framework into position and soon all was in order again. I recall that it was very hot doing that job.

Another awkward job on the Parcels was when we could not get water at Bromsgrove on the up trip. This meant stopping at Five Ways to fill up. The station was in a cutting with high brick walls. The water column was against the wall at the entrance to a tunnel. It was always very dark and difficult to see what you were doing. The reason for taking water was that there was no water supply at New Street on the up side and the next supply was at Tamworth troughs. So we had to take some if there was not enough water in the tank to get there.

Sometimes when getting near to Bath, on the return trip with the Parcels, the coal situation would be getting serious. Twice I have swept the tender clean and put all the coal onto the fire with just enough fire and steam to get to the shed.

While in this link some 0-4-4 tank 2P engines of the 1900 Class arrived. They were to replace the old 0-4-4 tank 1Ps. They seemed to be all right, but on trying them on the local trips they were found to be not so good. I think that my driver and I were the first set of Bath men to have one. We started off from Bath in the normal manner, but as soon as we got going it was found that it was impossible to maintain the boiler water level. We arrived at Bristol in a sorry state, but had managed to keep going. Returning to Bath was no better. On arrival at the loco shed my driver was asked by the foreman what he thought of these engines. From his report it was decided to stop and examine them. It was found that they were seriously overdue for a lot of maintenance work to valves and pistons and other things. When this was done these engines were a lot better and they did some good work while at Bath.

One day when working an 0-4-4 tank from Bristol at about 12-15pm I saw a small child in our track. I shouted to my driver who immediately stopped. How this child got there I do not not know. The track was in a cutting, with a three-foot retaining wall one side, and a ten-foot wall on the other side. Carrying this little boy, aged about two years, up the embankment, an express sped by in the other direction. I handed him over to a group of schoolgirls who knew him and said that they would take him to his home. I rejoined our train and we went on our way. We told no-one about this, and heard nothing more.

One day we were on a short job and were told to dispose of 4826, a new 5 Class that had arrived on a troop special from Chester to somewhere on the South Coast via the S&D. This engine was brand new and had just been run in after being built at Crewe. A tender-load of large briquettes had been burnt and the firebox was filled up to the brick-arch with spent ashes. I had to shovel an amount of these ashes out before I could get to the firebars so as to be able to lift them and put the rest of the ashes into the ash-pan. My driver was very helpful and used to rake this out while I dropped the ashes down. Never have I seen so much spent rubbish in a firebox after a day's work. The shed master came onto the engine and had a look to see if anything of new design had been put onto this engine as it had been allocated to Bath. It was when the Class 5 Stanier Blacks were being re-allocated to Bath.

During the war three brand new 3P 2-6-2 tank engines, Nos.179, 180 and 181, had been sent to replace the 2P engines of the 1900 Class at Bath. Two of these engines worked the Bath and Bristol local passenger trips while the other was put on the banker.

When the war finished I was promoted into the S&D goods link. Not having done any goods work for a number of years, to be put on the 2-8-0 7F S&D engines which worked the majority of the turns really gave me backache for a few trips. This link was called the "heavy link" and it was just that. It was not ordinary going, but real pounding going up the Mendip Hills.

Starting from Bath the gradient on the single-line section to Midford was uphill for two of the four miles to Midford. Then almost normal gradients to Radstock (ten miles from Bath). There was a loco depot at Radstock to provide shunting engines and bankers for the next eight miles uphill with the ruling gradient of 1/50 to Masbury. After Masbury it was eight miles downhill to Evercreech Junction with the ruling gradient of 1/50 except for a slight uphill break for a mile at Shepton Mallet. It was often a struggle to haul the trains up the banks, but often a work of art to control the trains going downhill. There were no vacuum-fitted goods trains allowed over the S&D and all braking was done by the engine and the brake van.

The full banker-assisted load over the 1 in 50 gradient for a 7F 2-8-0 was between 28 and 32 wagons of mineral (coal or stone). Of course this depended on the size and weight of the wagons.

Meanwhile, with coal being in short supply and industry wanting all that it could get, it was decided to convert some engines to burn oil. 4826 was sent away for conversion and when it returned 4830, also converted, came as well, allocated to Bath. These engines were put into the Pines workings.

Along with the other firemen in the S&D goods link, I had to learn about oil burning systems. The Mail double-home turn had been reinstated, and when our turn came to do this job we took one of these engines to Bournemouth for the Pines workings. Firing proved to be much cleaner and easier with oil than coal, and the locomotive responded well.

The other turns in the S&D goods were mostly from Bath to Evercreech Junction or Templecombe on an S&D 2-8-0 Class 7F. Sometimes on a local pick-up job we would get an 0-6-0 4F. The other jobs in the link were either preparing or disposing of these 7Fs and one or two engines from passenger turns, etc.

It was rumoured that Bath loco depot was one of the heaviest if not the heaviest shed on the system for using engine brake blocks. Whenever a 7F was fitted with a new set of brake-blocks, which were special and of a harder wearing material than the usual ones, these engines did one trip over the S&D; then on return the brakes were adjusted and after the next trip the engine blocks were changed but, although the tender brake was adjusted, these often went another trip or two.

Descending the bank with these trains from Masbury to Evercreech meant very heavy braking. On passing over the summit at Masbury the tender brake was applied by the fireman and the guard applied his brake also. The speed of the train was now controlled by the driver. There was only one let up in the descent and that was at Shepton Mallet about half way down. Here there was a slight uphill stretch for about one mile through the station. Most of the trains stopped at this point to take water.

When the descent was restarted the same thing happened on this second part. Now the brake-blocks were hot from the first descent and the braking power was not so effective. By using the brake more, the speed was controlled, but a profusion of sparks came from the brake-blocks and during the hours of darkness the countryside was illuminated. Eventually it was decided to try *Ferodo* brake-blocks on the engine, but still maintain the cast-iron type on the tender. Towards the end of 1943 this was done on 13801. I was not on this engine for a little while but everyone spoke highly of the brake. When I did have a trip I thought that it was definitely a much better brake, with no streams of fire from the hot engine brake-blocks, but with a strong smell of *Ferodo* instead of hot metal blocks. These locomotives had four steam brake cylinders, three for the engine and one, as usual, for the tender. Boiler pressure on these engines was 190 lbs. Eventually all the 7F Class were modified and had *Ferodo* brake-blocks on the engine but the metal brake-blocks remained on the tender.

Templecombe men worked towards Bath from Evercreech on a goods train on one turn only, and that was the up pick-up which changed footplates with the 5-50am down pick-up from Bath, except when on the night banking turn from Evercreech to Binegar. The goods service from Bath was worked by Bath men only. The only other men who worked on these 2-8-0 7F engines on the northern section were Radstock men who had a turn relieving the 3-30am ex-Bath goods men and also one to the quarries at Binegar; they then changed footplates with the 9-05am ex-Bath goods men and were finally relieved by a set of men who had travelled from Bath. These men eventually worked the Fitted to Bath. This was not actually a vacuum-fitted train in itself, but it conveyed wagons to Bath for the 9-15pm Bath to Birmingham, which was a vacuum-fitted train.

S&D goods link did most of the 7F turns, but the Midland goods link had two afternoon goods jobs, and the early Mail (Monday, Wednesday and Friday) double-home to Bourne-mouth over the S&D.

The turns done by the S&D goods link included the 3-30am Bath to Evercreech which was relieved at Binegar by Radstock men, after working a train of 40 empty wagons for stone traffic. The next goods over the S&D was the 5-50am, a station truck pick-up train which conveyed local goods, either separate articles or wagon loads of coal, timber, flour, or potatoes, or anything required to individual stations along the line. En route, it met a similar train from Templecombe and changed footplates, so that both were working their way back to base.

Next came the 9-05am, formerly the 7-50am, which went from Bath to Evercreech Junction and back. The 11-20am and 12-45pm (a Midland goods link turn) did so as well.

The next goods was the Market. This picked up and dropped off goods and finished up at Evercreech. The return working for this job was the 10-10pm from Evercreech and was the start of the night's full bank load workings. Sixty wagons were usual, some loaded, but mostly empties. Should there be a shortage of wagons at Bath, then if there were extra ones on hand at Binegar, another six would be picked up, making a total of 66 wagons through to Bath.

The train would have to stop at Binegar anyway to detach the banker which was a 3F 0-6-0, 3194 Class; either the Evercreech shunter or a banker from Templecombe would be the assistance. With a downhill break in gradient at Shepton Mallet it was not always straightforward working. When the train engine was over the first bank, the driver would close the regulator and the fireman would apply the tender brake to keep the train together. The banker would still be pushing, and eventually he would be pushing the whole of the train against the tender of the train engine. Should that not be felt then the train engine driver would know that all was not well with the banker, so the train would come quietly to a stand. Should there be something wrong then lights would appear, or should the banker be short of steam or water, then, when all was in order, the banker driver would sound his whistle and on reply the train would restart. Should the train be felt, then the fireman would take off the tender brake at a certain point and the driver would open the regulator and a dash would be made to charge up the second bank.

The next service from Bath was the 5-15pm. This was the Poole goods. Should there not be a full load for Poole from Bath, then Evercreech traffic would be sent, and put off there. If there was traffic at Evercreech for Poole it would be picked up. On this turn we used to go into Templecombe Lower, where the men brought our return train out and we changed over footplates.

The 7-15pm, 7-50pm and the 10-30pm goods from Bath went to Templecombe Upper yard where on getting our return load, we had to return to Evercreech Junction tender-first. This, in the depths of winter, was no joy ride. Some drivers had a weather protection sheet, which was usually a piece of sackcloth or canvas but home-made. Should a gale be blowing this often got torn and blown away. There were fittings for a storm sheet on a 7F Class, but the sheets got torn and were often a nuisance when not in use by getting in the way when a clinker shovel was used.

The Up Mail (9-35pm from Bournemouth West) was a goods train, but was called this because it was the return of the engine and men off the 2-40am Down Mail double-home. This train conveyed china clay from Poole to the Potteries. A fair load was made up from Poole, but a banker load was usual from Evercreech Junction.

During my absence from the goods scene, which was from 1941 until after the war, there had been several changes. For instance, the 8-,10- and 12-ton carrying capacity coal wagons had almost disappeared and were being replaced by 16-ton carrying capacity steel-constructed wagons. The smaller, wooden wagons were the former private owner wagons and it was found that standard wagons were more suitable and cheaper to maintain than repairing old wooden ones, even if wood was available, which often it was not. A good number of railway-owned common-user wagons had also been replaced with a similar type, but made of steel instead of wood. Of course the wagons that had not been centrally pooled were still around but these were special types and for specific use only anyway. The box vans were still in service and comprised of both vacuum and non-vacuum types. Much later they were all fitted with vacuum brakes or withdrawn. On 1st January 1948 the railways were nationalised, and most of the larger wooden wagons belonging to private owners which still remained in service were withdrawn within a few years, and replaced with 16-ton capacity steel wagons.

One day while working 40 empty wagons for coal traffic from Evercreech Junction to Radstock, and going over the usual varying gradients, there was a slight snatch from the rear as the train stretched out, with the guard applying his brake to get the couplings tight. We continued on our journey, but on reaching Radstock we found that this snatch had split the wagon headstock and the drawbar had been pulled out. It was a wooden wagon and in a worn state. The train was a mixture of steel and wooden wagons. If this wagon had been made of steel, then I doubt if this incident would have occurred.

The 5 Class 4-6-0 engines returned, but only 5440 of the pre-war allocation. Nos.4826, 4844, 4917, 4945, and 5056 came on the scene. No.4830 was also allocated, but not until the oil-burning period.

With the end of the war came the need for better conditions of service. The Railway Unions fought for a shorter working week. Eventually this was awarded. Instead of a 6-day week of 8 hours a day, this was to become an 11-day fortnight, of an 8-hour day for train crews and some other shift workers, but a 7 hour 20 minute-day for many other grades. Train crew rosters were amended to 5-day duties one week, with the other day's work going to a rest day set. This was usually a morning turn, and the next week would be a 6-day week. This meant extra sets of men required. A rest day relief link was formed to do these turns.

During the winter service this was ideal, but in the summer service there was a shortage of men so it was agreed on a local basis that men who had a scheduled rest day on Mondays, Fridays, and Saturdays would work their rest days to make up for the shortage of sets of men. For example, the 3-30am goods men, although officially on a rest day, would work the 3-15am to Bournemouth and back, while the rest day relief set would work the 3-35am to Bournemouth and back, as the 3-30am goods would be cancelled anyway. This eased the shortage quite considerably. During our time in the S&D goods link, my driver and I did many trips to Bournemouth and back while working on our rest days. Two of the engines that we had several times were a Class 5 No.5418, and a 2-6-0 Crab No.2903.

When the railways were nationalised it was decided that a survey was to be made of all engines on all railways as to their working abilities. This was called the Locomotive Exchange Programme. The S&D was not left out, and the 7F 2-8-0 Class engines were tested.

One Monday morning, the 11-20am with 53808 was tested. Driver Percy Bromley, my regular mate, and myself were on this turn. There were two locomotive Inspectors on board, Midland Inspector Jack Dowell and Southern Inspector Sam Smith. Both were keen to see what this engine would do.

One of a number of 2Ps allocated to Bath. This was the engine that I had on my first firing turn. (Lens of Sutton)

Three 2Ps coupled together; Nos.40634, 40563 and 40569, leaving Templecombe to take up assisting duties from Evercreech Junction to Bath on Bournemouth to the Midlands Saturday services over the Mendips. (Ken Arnott)

Midlands design 0-4-4 tank, No.58086, the type used for many years on the Bath to Bristol route. (Peter Pike)

A BR Standard Class 5, No.73050, at Evercreech Junction on a Bath to Bournemouth passenger train. (Peter Pike)

One of the Bath 2Ps, No.40601, on a branch passenger train at Evercreech Junction. (Peter Pike)

53

Castle Class. No.5071 Spitfire, heading a passenger working at Pilning. (Peter Pike)

No.46100 Royal Scot at Bath Green Park about to back onto an express and work to the Midlands.— (Ivo Peters)

Ken Baldwin (left) and I stand alongside No.73051 on 7th June 1954 in Green Park loco yard. (Ivo Peters)

'Pushing' the broken-down West Country Class, No.34041 Wilton, at Binegar on 1st August 1953. From left to right: O.S.Nock, Norman Down (Station Master), Mrs Down (nearly hidden), myself, Bert Clark (fitter's mate), George Adams (chief fitter), Mrs Nock, Miss Nock, Trevor Nock. (Ivo Peters)

No.13805, one of the 1914 series of S&D 7Fs. This was the first engine of this class that I worked on, both as a fireman and a driver. (Lens of Sutton)

0-6-2 No.5689 was one of the two bankers allocated to Westbury for work on the Warminster bank, along with No.6625. (Lens of Sutton)

One of the Moguls allocated to Westbury. I worked on this engine many times and twice it caused me a great deal of trouble. (Lens of Sutton)

No.5416, one of the auto-engines at Westbury which worked several of the branch passenger services. (Lens of Sutton)

No.4917 Crosswood Hall returning to Westbury from a tomato special to Woodford. Although a good engine, it was then withdrawn from service, a victim of dieselisation. (Lens of Sutton)

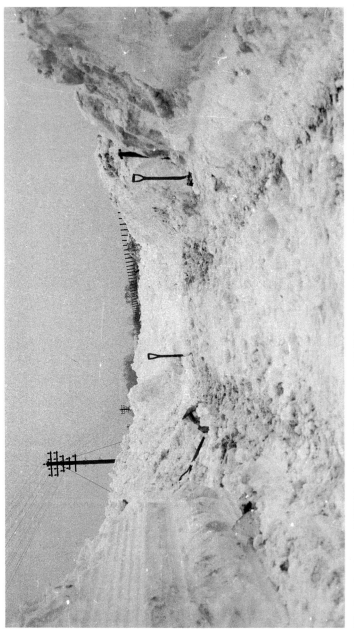

The harsh winter of 1963 is witnessed here on the S&D between Masbury and Binegar on 5th January. No train passed this point for five days. (John Stamp)

7F, No.53803, running into Shepton Mallet on the down line in January 1955. (John Stamp)

7F, No.53807, seen on the 1/50 gradient between Shepton Mallet and Cannards Grave cutting in January 1955. I have just fired the locomotive with smallish Welsh coal, all that was left on the tender after over ten hours in service. Most of the rake of 40 wagons were destined for Norton Hill Colliery where a full load would be picked up for Bath Gas Works. The photograph was taken by John Stamp who was the fireman on No.53803 about to pass on the down line. (John Stamp)

We both had a good idea of the outcome as this engine was not performing very well at this time. Off we set on our trip with a full load and kept a fair head of steam until passing Chilcompton when we began to get into trouble with steam and water. Approaching Binegar both the Inspectors asked the driver "What shall we do?". He asked me the same question, to which I replied "Stop and have a blow up", knowing that we did not have enough water in the boiler to go from a 1 in 50 uphill gradient, then close the regulator, and go to a 1 in 50 downhill gradient without the risk of uncovering and fusing the firebox fusible lead plugs. Percy agreed, then eased and closed the regulator. The banker knew what was about to take place as this often happened at that time when engines were short of steam and water. We came to a stand in Binegar station, and after a few minutes we put ourselves right for steam and water to proceed safely and set off again on our journey.

On reaching Shepton Mallet, while we took water the Inspectors examined the engine. What they found warranted the engine being stopped for repairs for several days when we returned to Bath. This engine when it returned into service was in a much better condition than before.

The following week we were on the 5-15pm Poole goods and had these Inspectors riding with us every night. They went through to Poole, and after two weeks had travelled on and examined every 7F on the S&D.

During the spring of 1950, I was told to prepare myself to see the Inspector for the examination to become passed for driving duties. This examination was to take place at Bath Locomotive Department. The day arrived and I got the examination room (which was the Mutual Improvement Class hut) warm and comfortable so that we could settle in and have our chat. As the whole of the S&D had recently been put into the Southern Region one of their Inspectors unexpectedly came along as well to see how the LMS conducted their examinations. I was asked if I objected to another Inspector being there. As I knew both of them previously I was quite at ease.

We started on the oral part and I was asked a multitude of questions, everything appertaining to the Rules and Regulations and various types of working conditions. Then came a multitude of questions about the steam locomotive and how everything worked, and a host of other things.

Then going outside the cabin and into the shed, as we walked around a spare engine I had to name all the parts that were pointed to and explain what they were and what was their purpose. I then had to make some oil feed trimmings. Finally I had to ask the foreman what engine I could oil as in preparing to work a trip, to the satisfaction of the Inspector. This examination, including a meal break, took about eight hours to complete.

I was then told that I had to have a trial trip the next day. This was to drive a passenger train from Bath to Evercreech Junction and return to Bath driving a goods train. The engines were 5440 on the passenger and 53805 on the goods.

The drivers on these jobs travelled in the brake vans during my trial trips. When we arrived back at Bath I was told that subject to my passing the medical examination, I was now a passed fireman. The next day I had the medical and was issued with all the books and forms that went with a driver's job. After signing the Road Card, stating all the routes over which I felt confident of driving a train, I then had to wait until I was required for a driving turn.

Within a few days I was booked out on a driving turn and had to prepare and dispose of a couple of engines. Then I was sent on a couple of trips to Bristol (Barrow Road) to get a couple of engines. I was then booked on a passenger turn.

Within a few weeks I was promoted into the Midland goods link as a fireman, where there was a vacancy.

Gloucester, to an LMS man, was Gloucester (Eastgate) station. Some time after nationalisation it was closed and has now disappeared. Unfortunately there were three level crossings between Tuffley and Gloucester (Painswick Road, California crossing and Barton Street). These of course halted road traffic. As there were no crossings on the GWR route going to the same destination this was the route chosen when one was eventually closed.

The former LMS Gloucester station and yard formed the changeover point for many of the goods trains booked over the ex-LMS route, both northwards and southwards. The relieved crews went to the relief cabin, and after reporting to the Control, eventually received their return workings. Meanwhile they had their meal break.

One day we were doing this when we were told to relieve a certain coal train at Tramway Junction going to Bath. It had a 2-6-0 Doodlebug of 43XXX Class on it. The men told us that they had not done very well in getting there, and had cleaned the fire and done their best. The fire-hole doors were closed. They went away relieved, in more ways than one. On looking into the firebox I saw a black mass, but a flame of light at each corner, where the firebox seams joined. On the tender was nothing but granulated American or Belgian small coal. Showing my driver the situation I asked his advice. He viewed the scene and was bound to admit that he had never seen anything like it, and I was to do what I thought best. It would have been hopeless to leave the siding in this state. We agreed that I should try to get something else from the Control. Proceeding to the signalbox to see what I could get, a light engine passed by going to Bristol. Having found this out from the signalman I asked him to tell the next signalman to hold it, as we wanted some help in our trouble. Whether they were ready to leave Gloucester station I do not know, but I told the Control of our plight, and they offered this engine to assist us towards Bristol. The signalman and I had a quiet grin to ourselves as the Control thought that it had been their idea. We dropped into the station behind this waiting engine. The men were not pleased at having to help us, but I told them that it had been the Control's idea, so they helped us until we got to Yate. We then continued to Bath on our own.

One night I was booked to drive on a Government special to Gloucester en route for Scotland. This train was to stop only for water and relief. We had engine No.44558, a 4F 0-6-0, and were told to coal the tender to capacity. We had 50 sheeted common-user wagons on the train. When the guard gave me the load the Inspector was there also. I asked what was on the train but they did not know except for the number of wagons and the weight. Off we went and arrived at Gloucester where we took water and had relief. I told the relief crew the conditions of working the train.

On walking past the train, going to the relief cabin, a wagon sheet tie was undone, so I pulled the sheet into its position and retied the rope, but to my surprise I saw what the load was; it was high explosives. We had our meal break, but I told no-one what was on the train.

About this time there was one trip that I think is worth mentioning. I was the fireman on the 2-00pm special goods Bath to Evercreech Junction. We had 48228, an 8F 2-8-0, and a full bank load. We turned over the summit at Masbury and I applied the tender hand-brake fully as usual, looking over the side to ensure that the tender wheels were not skidding. Emerging from Windsor Hill Tunnel I heard a skidding noise. I saw all the wheels were rotating, but still heard something was skidding. On looking again I saw that, although the wheels were rotating, the tyre of the middle wheel had stopped and was skidding. I shouted up to my driver, who immediately applied more steam power to the brakes, so that I was able to take off and reset the tender hand-brake.

In pre-Stanier days (on the LMS) the tyres on locomotives were studded onto the wheels. Now, with different ideas and designs, the tyres were affixed in a different manner. The excess heat generated on the tyres by heavy braking caused the tyres to become loose. When cooled the tyres shrank and were all right again. This was not serious in itself, but the fault was kept under observation and the pair of wheels were replaced at a convenient time.

Soon, in 1951, there was a vacancy for a deputy foreman at Bath, and I was asked to apply for this position. I did and was accepted. There were four deputies on the panel at Bath. It was during the winter service, and the coal stage was to be rebuilt. This meant that three of the deputies, one on each shift, would be constantly supervising the alternative arrangement for coaling engines by steam crane and bucket. I was given two nights' tuition by a deputy, then I had to take on the job myself owing to illness. This went on for several weeks until an opportunity came for me to learn the office side of the job. After two more weeks of tuition I was marked up to take charge and did the two turns of duty, 12-00 midnight to 8-00am and 4-00pm to 12-00 midnight, on alternate weeks, for a long while.

The 4-00pm foreman allocated all engines from 12-00pm to the next 12-00pm as far as possible, taking out all those wanted for boiler-washing and repairs, etc. The 12-00pm foreman and the 4-00pm foreman were in charge of the shed during that time, and had to see that all things ran smoothly. Each had to supply men and engines to work all trains, including specials, often at short notice.

I started the deputy foreman's duties during the winter service, and as it was the slack period I was able to settle in and have time for thought when planning certain moves. This gave me confidence to do the job.

A deputy foreman did the outside arranging job on a Saturday during the summer period. His job was to see that all engines were ready for their jobs, and in a position to be able to go into traffic quickly when required. The engines from arriving trains had to be turned, disposed of and coaled on the main shed.

My policy was to get all outgoing engines as far as possible into the sidings at the Midland shed, next to the main line and in order, coaled and watered so as to be able to go straight out to traffic when prepared, leaving the shed and loco yard as far as possible free for the incoming engines.

Engine failures were not welcomed, as there were never any spare engines or men. When they did occur it was sometimes possible however to re-arrange engine availability by moving engines onto an earlier job until something else became available.

Only once did I have an almost complete standstill of the service. As outside arranger I received news of an engine failure when it was being prepared. No engine was available on the loco for this job. It was midday on a very busy Saturday. Arrived from the Midlands with a Bournemouth special was a spare engine which I could use. As the engine arrived on the shed it was immediately pounced upon, and although it did not arrive on shed until 12-15pm it was turned around, coaled, watered, fire-cleaned, re-prepared and had left the shed by 12-55pm to work the train away without any delay. This quick turn round was achieved by three sets of loco men all working together, and the luck of having an engine with a "rocker" fire-grate. This job was done with a minimum of argument and upset. The booked time for this work should have been two hours for one set of men.

At Bath there were only two booked trains throughout the year on a Sunday. This was a tank engine local service on the Mangotsfield Branch. One train was in the morning and the other during the evening. These jobs were booked in the Midland passenger link. Any other Sunday work was done by passed firemen and passed cleaners.

During the summer service there was an excursion from Bristol to Bournemouth and back. This train left Bath at 10-15am hauled by a Class 5, and assisted to Shepton Mallet by a 2P, which then returned light engine to Bath. The same engine returned during the evening to Evercreech Junction to assist the return excursion train back to Bath.

I was lucky enough to be booked driving to Bournemouth on this job two or three times each year. We used to book on, engine prepared, and work to Bournemouth, calling at Radstock, Midsomer Norton, Shepton Mallet, Evercreech Junction, Blandford, Poole, and Bournemouth.

On arrival at Bournemouth, we had to dispose of the coaches and, turning the engine on the triangle at Branksome, we went onto the shed and disposed the engine and had our rest period. When it was time to think about returning we prepared the engine and worked back to Bath during the evening. After the train had gone on to Bristol, we took the engine to the loco, turned the engine and left it on the ash-pit. This train was well patronised, several passengers being railway staff and their families.

Another Sunday turn was when I was on a ballast train on the Midland route. Two 4F 0-6-0 engines were ordered and another passed fireman and myself, each having a passed cleaner as a fireman, went to Westerleigh for this train. In fact it was three trains; each train had 20 wagons of stone or sand, and an engineering brake-van at each end. This totalled 60 wagons and 6 brake-vans, all loose-coupled. I questioned the load, as it seemed to be a heavy lot to control over a falling gradient where we had to stop in Charfield loop. Everyone decided that it was all in order. We set off, but the downhill through Wickwar Tunnel and onward to Charfield proved this to be a very heavy load, though we did get there safely with this rather unusual load. The other engine went forward light engine and did its work in the section, while we pulled an excavator at a slow pace as it removed the redundant ballast, and put it onto the embankment. Eventually we were relieved and went home to Bath by road.

The next day I was booked up on a driving turn, assisting the Pines to Gloucester over the same track that I had worked on 24 hours before.

The last firing that I had to Avonmouth ended with having a rough trip. We had a full load on from Avonmouth to Bath. Although we were doing very well, the engine started to slip when we were part of the way through Clifton Down Tunnel. Sand was applied, but this seemed to have little effect. Although still moving we crawled very slowly out of the tunnel, and continued on our way. When we got to within sight of Kingswood Junction the engine slipped to a standstill. There was no sand left, so I had to walk to the signalbox and seek assistance. The banker from Barrow Road (Bristol) was sent to help, and we were assisted to Fishponds. The engine we had that night was the old stalwart 44417 of Templecombe.

During my career at Bath I went into and out of the S&D passenger link three or four times, the Midland passenger link three times, the S&D goods four times, and the Midland goods link three or four times. This may seem rather a lot of moves but, with retirements, men moving to other depots, whether for promotion other reasons, men going to or returning from their war service, or any other cause, all this made link moves necessary. When I was a passed fireman, I was on three different rates of pay. One rate was for firing duties, another for when I was doing driving duties, and yet another rate of pay for when I was doing foreman's duties. The pay clerk was a good man and I seldom had to call his attention to my pay account. One time he did pay me nearly twice as much as he should have, but we sorted out this mistake and I agreed to have this deducted from my wages packet on the next pay day.

Some while later I graduated into the spare link. This link was originally formed to cover all the rest days and was manned by the junior drivers and the senior firemen of the depot. There were six turns in this link. The firemen in this link were seldom on their booked job, as they were usually on a driving turn.

Some while after I went into this link it was decided to work the Southern West Country Class locos over the S&D. These engines had been tried before on a few trains, but Bath men knew nothing of this type. We were instructed on this class and were then able to work on them as required.

As Bath was now in the Southern Region, the Midland Region was no longer involved. It was decided that the supply of motive power over the S&D should be the responsibility of the Southern Region, and this region would be responsible for the supply of the extra engines required to work the summer service. The existing engines that were allocated would remain, on loan, until replacements could be found. Four West Country Class, Nos.34040, 34041, 34042 and 34043, were allocated to Bath. When 34043 went for overhaul 34044 replaced it. There were also three 4-6-0 BR Standard 5 Class engines allocated, numbered 73050, 73051 and 73052. These and other engines, working from the Bournemouth end of the Southern, helped out but no other engines, except what could be borrowed unofficially, were forthcoming from the Midland Region. This was not enough to run the required service on a Saturday. There was only one alternative and this was to press the S&D 2-8-0 7F engines into working some of these trains. Although we sometimes had to use these engines, I was reluctant to do so, as were the other foremen and deputy foremen.

On all the trips that I had, both firing and driving, I was never on an S&D 7F Class working a passenger train. When the shortage of engines made it impossible to run the service on a Saturday without using these engines, I had to book them on these trains many times when doing the deputy foreman's work. I was normally doing the job of outside arranging or on an express to the Midlands when these were being used on the Saturday specials.

I recall one Saturday morning being on the same train as my rostered driver. This was on one of the first Saturdays of the summer service. Two West Country Class locos were to work the 2-45am Bath to Bournemouth, which came in from the north. My rostered driver was on the assisting engine with a passed cleaner, while I was on the train engine with another passed cleaner. We both went through to Bournemouth with this train but came home with our same engines working different trains. Each of our return trains would have been a 12-coach load, but assisted from Evercreech Junction to Bath.

After a little while in this link it was decided, through a majority vote at a Locomotive Department committee meeting, that the links should be revised, and that the firemen should be in the same progression link order as the drivers. This meant that I would be put into the S&D passenger link, as I was amongst the six most senior firemen at the depot, and would do the same jobs that I had done ten years previously.

The turns were almost the same, but on a couple of jobs we changed over with men working the 76XXX Class engines which were allocated to Bournemouth.

There were several senior men to myself who had been made drivers at other nearby depots, and were waiting to return to Bath as drivers when a vacancy occurred. This made them next in line to become drivers at Bath. There were no foreseeable vacancies and I could see that it would a long time before I would become a driver at Bath. When the next vacancy list was posted I saw that there was a vacancy for a driver at Westbury, and that I could possibly get it. I made enquiries about everything concerning the place and what the work and jobs were, and I decided to apply for the position. I was successful.

My Driving Years
at Westbury

When I arrived at Westbury I alighted from the train and stood on the station platform looking around for the locomotive shed. Although I lived only 15 miles away I had only been through the station three times by train. All I knew of the railway and its work here was from what I had been told.

A young fireman also got off the train. He seemed to be going on duty, so I walked in the same direction. When we got to the shed I reported to the booking-on clerk, gave him my name and told him that I was the new lad. I was directed to the roster clerk's office, where I was given a full briefing as to what I would have to do as regards to hostel arrangements, registering with the council for a house, lodging allowances, what link I was to be placed in, and what road learning I had to do before I could take on the job.

Westbury Locomotive Department had 137 sets of footplate men, and I was to go into the junior goods and relief link. All progression links had 14 turns. Relief turns were to relieve train crews, and were not involved with preparing and disposing as on the Midland system. Disposing was done by fire-droppers, who did this job on the ash-pit, the engines being moved by footplate men, who were called shed turners.

Westbury, being an old GWR shed, worked entirely to their old system of working. There were many good points to this system, but there were also some antiquated ideas. The coal stage floor was in line with the coal wagon rail level instead of the wagon floor as at Bath. This meant that the coal could be scooped or slid out of the wagons instead of each shovelful having to be lifted to fill the tubs. This was much quicker and less laborious to operate than when the floor of the coal stage was at wagon floor height. On the other hand, if the ash-pits in the shed had been made another foot deeper, then a lot of drivers, myself included, and other staff with larger than average midriffs would have had less difficulty when getting under their engines.

All the engines allocated to Westbury were former GWR types. There were no Castles or Kings but should an engine from either of these classes fail and require a replacement from Westbury, then these engines, when repaired, would be worked away in service. Sometimes these would fail with a hot bearing and have to be lifted. It was in the fitting shop where all engines were lifted and new axle-box bearings fitted. In fact, if a King was lifted, the chimney was very near to the roof of the shop.

On the goods side, there were plenty of 28XX Class engines calling at the shed, but none were allocated until some while later. A 72XX tank engine, usually 7202, 7205 or 7242 off the Bassaleg and Salisbury coal train, was a daily visitor; it returned to South Wales in the evening on the Holt Junction to Penarth Curve with a train of coal empties.

My road learning, for a start, covered the station and yards at Westbury, then to Yeovil, Salisbury, Newbury via Lavington and also via Devizes, and to Bristol (North Somerset Junction). Of course all the sidings and yards at these places were included.

Road learning means that a driver, before he is allowed to take charge and drive a train over a specific section of track, must acquaint himself with all signals, points, catch points and crossings, all gradients and permanent speed restrictions, and any other matter concerning the safety of any train that he may be called upon to drive. He will then sign a Road Card in front of a witness acknowledging his competence and willingness to take charge over this route.

When my road learning over the Yeovil route was complete there was a booked turn in the link to work a goods train to Castle Cary on a Saturday night, then to bank any goods train up Bruton bank to Brewham. This I did with engine 5689, an 0-6-2 tank. No-one, except my fireman, knew that this was my first trip driving on a "Western" engine. The next week I finished learning the road to Salisbury. Then came a Sunday job to relieve a Bristol and Salisbury goods, also my booked turn. I did this job, and other booked turns came around which included the Sparkford goods which went to Yeovil, if required; the three banking turns up the Warminster bank; the 2-30am preparing turn; and any Salisbury jobs that were booked.

Soon I had learnt and signed for Newbury and Bristol (North Somerset Junction) and now I could do all the jobs in the link. There were several relief jobs where we relieved a train set, did a little job with the engine, and then took the engine to the shed.

One job lasted for several hours. We used to relieve a Reading set, turn the engine around on the triangle from Westbury station to Hawkridge then Heywood Road. We then picked up the slip coach that had been slipped off a Paddington and Plymouth express at Heywood Road, and brought it into Westbury for attaching to a Weymouth train. Then we used to take water, get the coal forward, put the engine right, and go light engine to Trowbridge, then couple the engine onto a passenger train in the bay sidings to go via the Devizes Branch to Reading. On being relieved we then went to Bath, as passengers, where we got aboard a light engine, a Hall Class, which had left Westbury 14 hours previously, and had done various trips to Exeter and back. We then took this engine to Westbury where we left it on the shed for disposal.

Another job in the link was, when required, to take an engine from Westbury loco and go tender first to Freshford and assist, with a 63XX Class 2-6-0, the Whitland Milk to Newbury. This was when the load was too heavy for the Hall or Castle over the Berks & Hants route. After getting to Newbury we would uncouple, turn the engine around and return light engine to Westbury.

There was also a turn where we manned a daily station truck train calling at all stations and sidings from Westbury to Sparkford, and sometimes Yeovil if required. This was with a 57XX Class 0-6-0 tank engine. We had to put off any wagons destined for these places en route, shunt and pick up any wagons, loaded or empty, for dispatch. This was both to and from Sparkford. When we arrived back at Frome we put off any empty wagons that were suitable for coal or stone traffic and made up to a full load of stone. This load was heavy to get away from Frome, but after getting over the summit at Clink Road Junction it could also be a difficult task to keep the train under control on the downhill grade to Fairwood Junction and so into Westbury.

These 57XX Class 0-6-0 tank engines were, in my opinion, the best tank engine that I ever worked on. They would deal with any local passenger train, local goods train, any passenger or goods shunting, or banking job that was allocated to them, provided that they were not overloaded.

An early morning turn in this link was a preparation job starting at 2-30am. This was a dirty job, and a special oversize overall coat was on hand for drivers. With this jacket on, a pocket full of corks (to plug oil reservoirs), a set of prickers (to remove broken corks), a few trimmings and an oversize oil-feeder and a flare lamp, both kept in a locker for personal use, and a wad of cotton waste, a driver was ready to have a go at oiling, and getting the three Hall or Castle Class and the three or four tank engines ready for service that he and his fireman were rostered to prepare.

My fireman and I had a system to which we worked and we often did not see each other for a long time while getting these engines ready; we could call to each other if needs be. When the way was clear we then went outside the shed and took water to finish the job.

Another part of this turn was for the driver to syringe the axle-boxes of the engines that had been washed out during the night. Several types of engines were prone to water leaking into their axle-boxes, especially tank engines. With a home-made syringe I was able to draw off this offending water and then to refill with oil. I was also able to gain a good knowledge of the construction of GWR engines while doing this turn. The only other compensation was that Saturday was the booked rest day.

There were three banking turns in this link, and they covered the whole day. Anything that wanted assistance up the bank towards Warminster, the banking engine did the job. There were two engines of the 0-6-2 Class shedded at Westbury; they were 5689 and 6625. Many times there was a struggle up the bank, when the train engine was not doing very well, but we always managed to get there.

One night a 63XX was the train engine on a train from Avonmouth to Salisbury. We started off, but about halfway up the bank, the train began to labour. I increased our effort more and more until we were at full power. We just managed to get over the summit and into Warminster. On unhooking the engine, the guard came back to the engine and thanked us for our effort, as he knew that we had been pushing most of the train. We whistled up to the train engine that all was in order at the rear, then after a little while the train moved off. We never did find out what was the trouble that gave us such a heavy trip.

The banker from Westbury went coupled to the train at all times, except during the day when the intermediate signalbox at Upton Scudamore was open; then the banker used to drop off at this place and cross over at the points, and return to Westbury. One morning we banked a goods train to Upton Scudamore and stopped over the points while the train proceeded. I sounded the engine whistle, but to my surprise I saw that the signalbox was still closed. The signalman had not arrived on duty. I then chased after the goods train with our engine, and on arrival at Warminster sounded the whistle. The signalman realised the position, let us into the platform and all was put right.

There were several drivers in the junior goods link that were keen on a bit of leg-pull. One day in the messroom one of them said that Midland men were not so good on the banker as Western men. He jokingly commented that when a Western man was on the banker he had to brush the smoke-box ash deposit from the banker off his doorstep every morning, but not so when a certain Midland man was on the night banker. I found out where he lived, about half a mile from the railway. When next I was on the night banker I obtained a strong brown paper bag that would hold a cubic foot of ash, tied and addressed it to this driver and placed the parcel on his doorstep early in the morning, with the message: "With the compliments of the night banking staff". The next time that we met he jokingly said that I was now banking like a true Western man.

A Castle failed at Heywood Road one night, and being on the banker, I was sent out to pull it into Westbury. We coupled up, and set about to pull the loco to the shed. I thought that we were pulling only the engine, but the whole parcels train of about 350 tons was still coupled up. However, we managed to pull the train into Westbury, and took the engine to the shed.

One Saturday afternoon, on the banker with a young fireman, I was told to take the engine to the shed. On arrival I was met by the foreman, who told us to take the pilot and go out to Heywood Road to assist a Kingswear and Paddington express to Newbury. We went out as instructed and coupled on in front. The train driver asked me to give him all the assistance I could, as they were very short of steam. Off we set, but I soon found out that my fireman was a passed cleaner and had only been on a local shunting engine in the few times that he had booked as a fireman. We had a Hall Class, and so I gave him instructions just as I had been told, about 27 years previously. Arriving at Newbury we were thanked by the train crew for our effort. We turned the engine, and returned to Westbury, pleased with the result of a good job done, and my mate pleased with the knowledge that he had fired a locomotive on an express. He became a fireman and progressed through the links, and is now a driver on expresses himself.

The next day I was on a 10-00am spare turn waiting for orders. Wanting something to occupy my time, I was looking at the Daily Alteration Sheet (a list of men altered from their booked turn, or spare men booked out on specials, or train jobs, or any other reason why men were not on their rostered jobs). When someone in civilian clothes said to me: "You turned those wheels around pretty smartly yesterday, didn't you?", I replied "The passengers like to get home on time if possible, don't they?" I was then told that it was a good effort. On making enquiries I was told that this man was the Shed Master. A few minutes later he saw me again and asked if I had ever thought of doing the deputy foreman's work as there was a vacancy at the depot. I told him that I had filled this position at Bath for four years before my transfer to Westbury. I was now living near to the shed and would not mind having a go at these duties as I liked the challenge.

The Superintendent interviewed me and I was accepted. I was given an insight of the system, and a few days later was booked up to do the job, as and when required. This lasted for at least the next ten years at Westbury.

There were a few drivers at Westbury that were against a Midland man coming to a Western shed. One driver was very scornful. One day in the messroom he asked me, no doubt egged on by the cabin crowd: "Why did you come to Westbury?" to which I replied, "I did not really want to come, but I was sent as a missionary amonst all you heathens". Laughter broke out amongst the men as they knew what sort of a person he was. Not being content with this result he came back with a complaint of silly Midland ideas being put on BR engines. I asked him to explain, which he did and I was able to tell him that his complaint was from a Southern idea. Again laughter from the men. After this episode we became firm friends and never again had a mis-word.

One night I was doing the 10-00pm to 6-00am foreman's duties and had to give a repair card to the bar boy. This firebox job was his work and I wanted this engine for an early morning job. Soon he returned the card and told me that the job could not be done. I quietly had a look at the repair and could not see why it could not be put right. I casually met the bar boy and asked him what was the difficulty. He explained, so we went to have a look together, though I took a tool that I knew would be required. He gave his explanation, and then I asked him if I might have a go at doing the repair. The repair was put right and the engine went on the job where I had booked it. He admitted that he had never seen this done before, and asked me how I knew this type of work. I had to admit to him that I had done all types of firebox work, and all other shed duties, when I had started on the railway nearly 30 years before.

One of my first jobs after taking on as a driver was on a ballast train on a Sunday. We were marked spare, but an extra engine was required at Seend. The foreman gave us the job, but although I had heard of, and had seen the place, I could not recall where it was. When we walked towards the engine I asked my fireman where Seend was, and he told me. Of course I knew then where it was, between Holt and Devizes. We got there on a 0-6-0 Pannier Tank 4636 and were asked to attempt to pull rails, in pairs, onto a secured bogie bolster by means of wire ropes hooked onto the rail ends and with the other end attached to the engine drawbar, with the ropes running over a roller at the end of the wagon and along the floor of the wagon. Although I had never done this job before I had a go and we did it with no difficulty. My fireman gave me confidence by saying that by doing this job we had saved many hours of heavy lifting by the platelaying gang. Several lengths of rails were loaded until the wagon was full.

Another turn in this link was an 11-00pm shed turning job. All the engines that arrived for reservicing were left on or near the ash-pit. As the fires, ash-pans and smokeboxes were cleaned and cleared, the engines were then moved to get coal. Normally every engine was coaled reasonably full, with those going to South Wales not so full, as it was not practical to send spare coal back whence it came. When this was done they had to be put into the shed after they had been turned around in readiness for their next job or any repairs that were needed.

All the shunting turns, both at Westbury and the one at Trowbridge, as well as the local branch passenger turns, were covered by the spare turns, so although there were several turns in the link there were often not many spare men available.

After some time in this link I was promoted into the senior goods and relief link. This meant more road learning. I had now to learn Weymouth, Taunton, Reading, Swindon and Severn Tunnel Junction.

The road to Weymouth and Reading was the first, but Taunton was more difficult as beside the Castle Cary to Taunton direct route, I had to learn the stretch between Athelney and Cogload via Durston as the auto service went over this route. To do this I had to book on early and catch the 6-25am from Westbury, or go to Yeovil at a more suitable time and get a branch passenger to Taunton which eventually went over this route. The route that this train took was, incidently, the main line before the Castle Cary to Cogload line was built.

Swindon with its large works and multitude of sidings needed a bit of sorting out, but in the end it was done. Severn

Tunnel was the next and this also was a bit of a teaser. The passenger side was all right, but the goods working was a little more difficult. There are several rules and regulations to be observed when working through the tunnel.

One trip on a goods train through the tunnel was of interest. I had been through the tunnel on a goods from Bristol, and had got onto a return train. This was a Midland 8F 2-8-0, and had a Severn Tunnel crew. The banker crew was, as always, from the same depot, and was ready to go. While waiting, both crews were having a chat at the side of the engines; I was on the engine having a quiet sandwich. When the road was set and the signal lowered, we started away. The train gathered speed and went rather quicker than I thought was normal. The engine began to shake, rattle and roll so I stood on the tender footplate, as this is a better riding position on a rough rider. When we got to the other end, both the crew looked at me and asked what I thought of the trip. I replied that although I had been comfortable I was sorry for the ride that they had been subjected to on a rough engine. They again asked if I was all right as they had gone at that speed for my benefit. I then re-marked that as an ex-Midland man I was used to these engines since before the war, and had been on even rougher engines than this many times. I then assumed that their little prank had misfired.

Another turn at Westbury was the Hoo Cement train that came from Hoo (south of the Thames and east of London) for Magor, the next station west of Severn Tunnel. It was a train of vacuum-fitted tank wagons of cement, and was equal to 95 wagons of goods traffic in weight. This train had only 25 wagons on for a full load. On relieving Salisbury men at Westbury we used to work, with a 28XX Class 2-8-0, via Bristol, and bank up Stapleton Road bank to Filton; then down the bank to Pilton, where a banker was attached in front to go through the tunnel.

One morning all was going well when the banker came onto the front. My mate asked me what was the load so that he could tell the driver while the fireman coupled up. I told him, and to say that they were a heavy lot. The reply that he got was "All right, boyo, we know" in his Welsh accent. Off we started towards the tunnel. The banking driver is always in charge of the train, and the train engine driver does not interfere with the working of the train until called upon, by whistle code from the banking driver, to help pull the train out of the tunnel, except in the case of an emergency.

In our opinion we were going too slowly, taking into consideration the weight of the train and the 1 in 90 uphill gradient at the Welsh end of the tunnel. I looked into the firebox and suggested to my mate that he should feed the fire with several shovelfuls of coal as I would have to work the engine extra heavy if we were to get this train out of the tunnel. Eventually the banking driver opened up, but before long he was in trouble. He whistled up for me to open up, but he then became short of steam. I had to use my ejector to keep the brakes off, and as he became weaker I had to work my engine very heavy. As we got out of the tunnel we were pulling most of the train. When we got to Severn Tunnel Junction station the crew came back and thanked us for our effort in their hour of need. They admitted that they had not assisted this train before, but they knew now that they were a heavy lot.

The next day with the same weight of train we had the same banking set. My mate asked me what fire we should need to go through the tunnel. I told him that we should have no trouble today. We started off and went through the tunnel like a passenger train with no trouble. We took the train, as usual, to Magor and back light engine to Severn Tunnel shed.

One of the turns in this link was the return working of a "trials" engine. These engines were running in after being released from having a general overhaul at the Swindon factory. They arrived at Westbury on the 4-30am goods from Swindon, and returned on the 1-30pm goods from Westbury to Swindon. Everything was tight and stiff to operate. I used to oil all the parts that I had to use as on this trip there was often a lot of shunting to do. This oiling assisted, and allowed easier working.

At one place we all too often picked up wagons of live ammunition. This type of traffic, with an untried engine, did not make things very comfortable. We were always glad to get rid of this cargo in Swindon yard and get to the shed. There were various types of engines on this turn. It could be a 28XX, a 72XX, a Hall, a Castle, or a 53XX. We often had these engines for about three days, according to how they were settling in. Care was always taken when working these engines to examine them whenever possible to see that all was in order.

On an early morning turn, the 4-40am Westbury and Weymouth goods, we were booked (when required in the tomato season) to work a special back to Westbury with our engine. Our engine would, in any case, be changed at Westbury and something else would work the train forward towards the Midlands. We had a 53XX Class this particular day, and it was a rough rider. Going down Evershot bank we were hopping about a bit, when my regular mate came over to my side and said that he was not riding over on his side. I asked him what was the trouble and he said that a lot of sparks were playing along the footplate. Seeing that the line was clear, I had a look, and sure enough there were showers of sparks. We stopped at Yetminster and removed the wheel splasher which had collapsed onto the wheel tyre and causing the sparks. We went on to Westbury, took the engine to the shed, where the engine was serviced and the offending splasher rebolted into position.

Westbury men often relieved specials and excursions that were for Weymouth. Often on these trains we had to book off on a short-rest basis, then prepare and work the return train back to Westbury at night.

The Channel Islands boat trains from Paddington going to and from Weymouth were always relieved at Heywood Road by Westbury men. The job was non-stop to Weymouth, taking water on the troughs at Fairwood, and pausing at Yetminster for a banker up Evershot bank, assisting at the rear but not being coupled up. With a Castle Class engine on the front it was found that the banker was often hard pressed to keep up. Looking back along the train as we were about to enter Evershot Tunnel we sometimes saw that there was a gap between the last coach and the banker. On arrival at Weymouth we uncoupled from the train and a tank engine took it through the streets and along the harbour walls to the quay. The up boat train followed the same procedure at Weymouth, but in the reverse order.

After the engine had been disposed of and the fire cleaned, we had by that time had our meal break, so we re-prepared the engine and waited for the train to be brought from the quay. When all was ready we used to couple up and away to Heywood Road with a banker assisting from Weymouth, through Bincombe Tunnel to the summit of the bank, which was a little way in advance. The banker was not coupled to the train so there was no need for us to stop. We took water on Fairwood troughs, so that when the Old Oak men relieved us it was all right to go on to London .

With some of the excursions, especially on a Sunday, we used to be booked to remain at Weymouth and work the train home during the evening. Sometimes, if the period of time was too great then we would be booked to return home and another set would travel to work the return train.

There was also a daily stopping passenger service, and should the crew be unavailable then a set in the spare link would be booked to cover these jobs. The usual engine for these jobs would be either a Hall Class, or a 63XX, normally 6399, 7300 or 7302. All these were engines allocated to Westbury. To work a passenger train which called at all stations and halts between Westbury and Weymouth, and back, was a good day's work for a fireman. The normal load was about five coaches and maybe a couple of parcels vans. The several halts that existed were difficult to find during the hours of darkness, and as there was no staff then the guard had to ensure that all was well before he allowed the train to proceed. During the winter period these jobs were cold and miserable and not very pleasant for the train crews.

During the pigeon season we were sent to Weymouth once to get a train of vans that contained empty pigeon baskets returning to the Midlands. We got the engine ready and went out to Jubilee sidings (where I had visited on a pigeon special about 20 years previously as a fireman from the S&D route via Broadstone). We set off with a few vans on, but on arriving at Dorchester we had to pick up several more vans that were in Cemetery sidings. This made a total of, I believe, 19 parcels vans on the train. Arriving at Yeovil we were told that there was a delay, as there was a derailment. Eventually we got to the station and were told that we could just get over the points with our load of 9 vans. When I reminded them that we had 19 on and not 9, they were amazed as we were unable to cross over to the other track with this number of vans on. It was decided that we might just be able to squeeze past the derailment very slowly as there was the minimum of clearance. We tried and did so. This was the only way to get by and to continue our journey.

Another trip that did not go entirely as planned was on a fully vacuumed goods from the West of England to London. It was about 2-00am on Sunday morning. We had relieved the crew at Taunton. The engine was a Hall Class, and the first stop was to be Heywood Road for relief. We were going along in fine fettle and about three miles short of Castle Cary when the brake was applied and we came to a stand. Looking back we could see nothing amiss. I told my fireman, who was my regular mate, to have a rest and to look after the engine, while I sorted out the trouble. Walking back alongside the train, I came to the 22nd wagon and heard the sound of air being drawn into the vacuum pipe. This pipe had fractured at an elbow joint. Disconnecting the vacuum pipe with the wagon on the engine side of this wagon, I was able to regain the brake on the front portion. Before we could continue the rear portion would have to made into non-vacuum braked stock.

The guard had joined me in his endeavour to find out the cause of the trouble, so we both made the whole of the train, from behind the defective wagon, into non-braked stock. This was soon done and we went forward as a partly-fitted train. This was permissible, but we stopped at Castle Cary to inform the signalman of our delay and what we were doing. We proceeded, but travelling at a slower speed owing to the brake power not being so effective. Of course the guard's van then carried side lights, and the engine carried reduced headlight code. The Control was advised and everyone was happy.

As and when required I was put on deputy foreman's duties. This, I might add, was not without its moments of excitement. One Saturday morning during the summer period I was just about to have a cup of tea, as everything was in order, when the phone rang. The message from the Control was: "The

Paddington and Plymouth passing Savernake wants a fresh engine from Westbury". Glancing for the number of the stand-by pilot the phone rang again. "Kingswear and Paddington passing Castle Cary wants a fresh engine at Westbury" was the message again from the Control. I went towards the messroom, but as I passed by the time office the clerk shouted: "The Cardiff and Salisbury is passing Bathampton and wants a fresh engine at Westbury". Going into the messroom I told one set of spare men to take the stand-by pilot out and change engines on the Kingswear to London train. To another set I told them to take an engine that had been prepared for a job leaving the loco in about two hours time, and change with the London and Plymouth train. Then to another set I told them to take a BR Standard 4-6-0 73XXX Class, which had just come onto the shed from Weymouth but had not been disposed of, to turn it and change the Cardiff and Salisbury.

I told each of these sets to get all the particulars that were required from the drivers so that I could make out the failure forms. I would have to make out five forms for each failure. To replace the engines that I had now used I told another spare set to get a fresh stand-by pilot ready, and to another set I told them to get an engine ready to replace the prepared engine that I had used for one of the failures. The messroom had been full before I had received my orders, and now it was virtually empty. There was also an engine to find to return to Weymouth to replace the one that I had also used.

The Saturday workings at Westbury warranted a foreman as a Supervisor at the station. Besides arranging for a banker to assist anything up the Warminster bank, he had to note that all trains passing through Westbury station were in order. One Saturday I was advised that a Cardiff and Salisbury passenger would require a banker, so I informed the banker driver of this job and was returning to the station office when this train came into view. As the driver closed the regulator I heard a noise from this engine that spelt trouble. I dashed into the Control office and said: "Advise the loco that a fresh engine is wanted on the Cardiff and Salisbury just running in".

They were amazed how I knew. As the engine passed by, the driver shouted to me "banker wanted". I replied: "and a fresh engine" and dashed to where the train was stopping in Westbury station. The driver got off and we found that the left big end was hot and the metal had fused. After the station work had been completed, I rode on the footplate to Westbury South signalbox where the engine was uncoupled and went towards the loco shed where the engine was exchanged. This fresh engine was off the Weymouth passenger and had been turned around before being disposed, and was waiting. The crews changed over and the train proceeded to Salisbury. This was also a BR 73XXX Class 5.

One afternoon doing the deputy's job, I received a phone call that the Salisbury and Cardiff passenger had failed when about to run into Warminster. I called for a fitter and his mate, and asking the Control to send these men on the banker to see what could be done. The stand-by pilot was also sent tender-first, to change engines if required and to work the train forward. The banker, with the fitter's approval, was able to pull the failed engine and train into Warminster, uncouple the engine from the train, and put both engines into the sidings. The stand-by pilot then coupled onto the train and changed footplates with the failed engine's crew who then worked the train forward to Cardiff. Meanwhile I arranged for another stand-by pilot to be got ready on the shed. It turned out that a piston valve had broken between the two heads. The banker pulled the failed engine to Westbury, where it was disposed of and a new valve fitted, either at Westbury or at Swindon.

Engines that had new bearings fitted at Westbury were often run in on local trips. At one time we had a trials engine that failed on a train. I was doing the foreman's job and one of these engines was on a local passenger train from Swindon to Westbury. At Holt it had a "hot box". The driver phoned me and I called on the shift fitter who told him to "baste" the hot axle-box with thick oil and to come on at a reduced speed if it got no worse. It was the right back tender axle-box.

When the engine got onto Westbury shed the men asked for another engine, but I told them to have their meal break, as the fitter would have a look at it. The fitter and his mate jacked up the tender of this 63XX Class and took out the bearing. The metal had fused, but the axle was all right. There was a new bearing in the fitting shop that was to be used the following day on another tender and had just arrived. The fitter's mate wiped everything perfectly clean, while the fitter got the new brass and fitted it to the axle by scraping and bedding in, making sure that it was a perfect fit. Then with a new axle-box oil pad and ensuring that everything was well oiled, all was reassembled. When I told the crew what had been done and that they could take the same engine home on their return working they were very surprised. The Swindon Trials fitters had to be informed of what had happened, and that Westbury wanted a replacement axle-box bearing. They assured us that one would arrive in time for the next morning's shift. It was duly supplied and all was again in order.

One afternoon, when on a spare turn, I was sent with 4636, an 0-6-0 Pannier Tank, to Melksham to change over with 2268, an 0-6-0 tender engine that was on a local goods turn. It had become derailed on all wheels and the breakdown gang was there doing their job. We changed over with the men of the derailed engine who went on their way to their next calling point. Eventually the engine was rerailed, but the tender was still off the track, and parted from the engine. I was called upon to move the engine out of the way, under its own steam, across the main line and into the cattle-pen siding. There was not much water in the boiler and this had to be replenished. The tender, with the water and coal, was on the other side of the main line. Finding the hose-pipe that was used to clean out cattle wagons, we connected it to a water supply and were able, with some paper packing, to connect the nozzle to the injector water supply pipe and so refill the boiler by adjusting the tap of the water supply to the injector's requirements. The Inspector in charge of the breakdown remarked that he had never seen this done before. Eventually the tender was re-railed and we were able to join up with the engine and return to Westbury.

On this class, the engine had a steam brake, but the tender had only a vacuum brake, although both worked off the same brake valve.

After the cement works opened at Westbury a train of empty vans had been put into the sidings and loaded. The full train had now to be taken away for dispatch. We had returned from the Sparkford goods turn and were sent to do this. The engine on this job was 9668, an 0-6-0 Pannier Tank. This was the first train of cement to leave these works.

It was during the winter period and snow, ice, frost and cold winds were very much in evidence. We were on a pick-up goods turn to Marlborough. This was from Westbury via Lavington and Savernake. The engine was 4172, a 2-6-2 tank. There was no water supply at Savernake so arrangements had been made for us to go from Patney to Devizes for water.

On arrival at Patney it was found that the points were frozen and could not be used. We were then told that Hungerford was the next supply. Before we arrived at Savernake all our water had been used. When we did arrive at Savernake we told the Control that we did not have enough water to get to Hungerford. They told me to throw out the fire, but as the boiler water level was safe, at least for a little while, I decided to have a look around and try to find out why there was no water supply before throwing out the fire. I looked at the water control panel, but could see nothing amiss. I then looked into the reservoir tank and saw that there was a sheet of ice where the full water level should have been, but when I tested it the ice broke and the tank was empty. The water supply valve control wires were frozen to the side of the tank, thereby making the supply valve inoperative and making it seem that the tank was full when in fact it was empty. I got into the tank as there was an iron ladder, both on the outside and on the inside of the tank. Knocking the ice from the wires they soon broke free and the floatweights lowered with a clunk. This opened the water valve, and there came a gushing sound as the water rushed in. I scrambled out of the tank just in time.

Leaving the reservoir tank to fill I went to tell the signalman what I had done. When the line was clear it was decided to try for water, and much to the relief of everyone water was now being delivered. After refilling our engine water tank and making up the fire, we carried on and went to Marlborough and did our work. We used this water supply every day that week, and the "No Water" notice as displayed at loco depots, was cancelled.

While in this link there were a couple of jobs that came to Westbury. One was for an empty coal train between London and South Wales, but we were to work it from Reading to Swindon. The other was a passenger job from Westbury to Swindon, then to go light engine to Newbury via Didcot to work a passenger train to Westbury. This involved learning the "Gold Coast" (the name given to the Didcot and Newbury branch). The whole of our link had to learn this route. This branch was one leg of a triangle covering Didcot, Reading and Newbury. Each leg was 17 miles long. The only trains that I could get to ride on over this branch were goods trains, and these were often going between Didcot and the Southern, and were of the Southern Q1 0-6-0 type; they were called "Ugly Ducklings". Eventually I learnt these roads, and worked many of the trains of empties, from Reading to Swindon, often with an LMS type 8F 2-8-0 that had been built by the Western at Swindon.

The links at Westbury were changed around, and I found that I had missed a link which did all their work under the direction of the Control, and was placed into the "super spare" link. This link was the cover for the long-distance express freight and express passenger work. Although there was some of this work rostered in the link, it also covered all the special trains of this nature.

The first thing that I had to do was to learn the road to London. This was the biggest headache of all. The road from Reading to Paddington was mostly semaphore and was a bit of an eye-opener to a person who had never done any work over this section. There were a minimum of four running roads from Challow to London, but with a greater density of traffic between Reading and Paddington.

There were also several crossovers and sidings along the way. Each of the many signalboxes, often at short intervals, had their own series of signals, making each into a short section. The two running lines on the left going towards London were the up and down relief lines, while the two running lines towards the right were the up and down main lines. Although all these lines could be used by any train the main lines were usually kept for expresses and the faster trains when they were running. Local passenger and slower trains generally used the relief lines.

There were two of us drivers from the same link marked to learn the road, so we decided to do this together. We both knew and signed the road to Reading so we travelled each day as passengers to Reading and asked permission to ride on the engine of an express to Paddington, normally the one that had brought our train from Westbury. This train was booked up the main line. On arrival at Paddington we got off and caught a DMU and by sitting behind the driver, but in the train, went down the relief line back to Reading, taking notes of all that we could see and what would be useful to us. At Reading we had a meal break in the canteen, then went back again to Paddington on another DMU, also on the relief line. We then sought out an express and again asked permission from the driver to go back to Reading on the main line, where we got off.

Travelling home to Westbury often in the same train, we had a chat about all the things that we had seen, and compared our notes on all that we learnt on that and previous days over this route, so forming a picture in our memory that would enable us to drive trains confidently over this route.

We did make changes to our routine when we decided to have a look at various other sites, such as Acton yard, Old Oak carriage sidings, and Old Oak loco depot. Should it be a fine day, maybe we would travel as far as Ealing and then walk along the side of the track to Acton yard, keeping well clear of any trains or wagon movements but stopping to look at various signals, points and crossings, and sorting out the whys and wherefores of these items. We would then eventually find ourselves at Old Oak carriage sidings where we would get a ride to Paddington while still learning the road as we had to learn the up & down engine and carriage lines which went between Old Oak and Paddington. We made several trips on engines between Paddington and Old Oak loco depot and back over the engine lines, as we would also have to do this movement in our bookings.

After four weeks of this road learning I decided to sign for the road. The roster clerk was very delighted when I did this as the driver of the 8-40am Westbury and Paddington passenger for the following day had gone sick, and he was searching for a driver to fill this turn. This was fortunate for him and I was booked on the job.

The next morning I prepared 6994 *Baggrave Hall*, but the fireman did not turn up for work as he was also sick. A young fireman was sent out to do the job, but although he was willing, he was unable to keep on the top side of the job. My road learning colleague, still learning the road, would be riding in the train and intended to join us at Reading. As we got towards Savernake I could see that my fireman was in difficulties and needed asistance. I went back to my colleague and explained the situation and that we were in trouble. He immediately offered to assist and came aboard. He gave my mate a rest and took over the firing. He was a good fireman and soon all was well. When we left Reading he came across to me and jokingly said "If you are late into Paddington I will tell everyone that you can't do the job". We arrived three minutes early. He came across again, and with a pat on the back said "Jolly good show". My fireman, inexperienced as he was, watched every move that was made. He learnt a great deal and also enjoyed the trip.

We found out later that this was his first trip on an express. On such a trip as this I was sorry that I could not assist him. This being my first trip over this route on my own, I had my hands full doing my own job. This was the first of many trips to London, both via the Berks & Hants, and the Melksham and Swindon routes.

In this super spare link were several booked jobs to and from London. I recall that one job was the Tavistock Junction vans. A 47XX Class 2-8-0, with 25 empty newspaper and parcels vans returning to Old Oak carriage sidings, formed the train. We used to relieve this train at Westbury and work it forward. By the time we arrived at London the engine was getting very tired. It was quite a job to propel this train up the slight gradient of the carriage line into the sidings.

When the signal was lowered for us to push back into the sidings a Tannoy loudspeaker called: "Right, Westbury men into H sidings, clear road". There were, at that time, 52 sidings in Old Oak carriage sidings, (including the Royal Train sidings). After detaching the vans the engine was then taken to the loco and left for servicing. This engine, or another of the same class, was then prepared to work the 9-25pm goods from Paddington to Plymouth. On this turn Westbury men would be at "Lord Hill's", a shunter's cabin for Paddington goods, to relieve the Old Oak men. With the few wagons we would go to Old Oak down goods yard, and make up to a full load. This load was, I believe, equal to 80 wagons of Class 3 traffic, though the length of the train could be no longer than 60 standard wagons, fitted throughout with a vacuum brake. We then worked this train, which was now the 10-40pm Old Oak goods to Plymouth via Westbury.

When the train was complete and ready to leave, the guard's van used to be against the buffers at the London end of the yard, while our engine would be just clear of the signal at Friars Junction, waiting to go onto the main line. The last DMU from Paddington to Reading used to go by on the relief line as we were leaving the sidings, but making limited stops en route. There was a belief by drivers, that if our train did not pass this DMU before it got to Slough, then we would be losing time. Whether this was true or not I cannot say, but we were certainly timed very sharp. This type of non-stop fully-fitted freight train was known in railway jargon as a "hard hitter". It was no use to put an inexperienced fireman on a job of this nature.

The line was very busy at this time of the night and there was a continuous flow of trains. Often the Distant signals were at caution until we were about to pass them. If they remained at caution then the brake would have to be applied severely and the speed reduced to be able to stop at the first stop signal if it was at danger.

Usually the train in front would be making good progress and we could run at a speed to keep our distance behind it. Eventually this train would get away, or would be diverted. Then we would get a clear run through Reading, and take water on Aldermaston troughs. Our first stop was Heywood Road where we were relieved by Laira men from Plymouth.

Another turn about this time of day was the 9-50pm Paddington to Penzance Parcels. We used to travel as passengers to Old Oak Common loco and take to a previously prepared engine, usually a Castle. Going tender-first down the engine and carriage line we would arrive at the Parcels Department. There we used to join up on each of the two roads and start away, with the first stop again Heywood Road as we took water on Aldermaston troughs.

One night we took 1003 *County of Wiltshire* from Old Oak shed for this parcels turn. There were two Westbury drivers learning the road with us. Knowing that they were almost ready to sign for the road I told them to have a go at the driving, while I kept my eye on them and stood out of the way in the corner on the fireman's side. The fire was very heavy and wanted lifting, so I did this for my mate to help him where I could. Off we started and were doing well, but on passing West Drayton I saw some sparks coming from under the engine. I shouted to the road-learning drivers who saw the same thing their side. I told them to stop and examine at Iver signalbox. On doing so the signalman said "You can't stop here", but by that time we had got down and found the cause of the trouble. The fire-grate had collapsed into the ash-pan and the ash-pan was melting. I told the signalman "All speed to Slough loco, engine failure". We went to Slough and into the sidings, uncoupled from the train and went into the loco depot. On the ash-pit I opened the hopper ash-pan, and the fire and firebars were dumped into the ash-pit. Unfortunately this pit had a spillage of diesel oil from re-fuelling DMU sets. This caught fire, but only for a few minutes. We moved our now fire-less engine into the shed.

The foreman came onto the scene and told us that the only spare engine that he had was a 94XX Class, 0-6-0 tank engine. This we took onto the train and proceeded to Reading. There the down line pilot was waiting to change engines. This was a run-down Hall that was waiting to be called into Swindon works for a general overhaul. We went onto Westbury with this engine where we were relieved by Laira men, who went on to Plymouth with the train.

I recall that the St Erth to Wood Lane milk tank train, before I went into the link, was a King Class job with a load of 510 tons. When I was promoted into the super spare link, the Kings were withdrawn. The engines that replaced them on these trains were Halls, as the traffic was easing off and not so heavy. After relieving the West of England crew at at Westbury we then worked the milk tanks and produce train to Acton yard where we dropped off the Smithfield Market traffic and then went on to Wood Lane (Olympia) with the milk tanks. We then returned to Westbury light engine, turning the engine on a triangle, North Pole Junction via West London Carriage sidings and onto the main line at Ladbrook Grove. We took water at the sidings.

One night we were put onto Southall loco with this engine to pick up and haul a dead 2-6-2 tank engine to Westbury with a "rider" (a fireman riding on the dead engine to ensure that everything remained in order on the engine, and to apply the brake in case of emergency). This engine was going for repairs at Newton Abbot factory.

Besides having a 47XX Class over the Berks & Hants on the West of England turns, we also had these engines over this route when thetrain known as the Up Cocoa, and the return job, were diverted from going via Swindon. The up train used to convey a full load of goods, much of this tobacco and cocoa. These were the products of the Bristol tobacco and chocolate factories. Westbury men used to relieve these sets of Bristol men at Hawkridge and work to Reading. The return working was the down part of this diverted train also via Hawkridge, and we were then relieved at Hawkridge by another Westbury set who worked the train to Bristol (Kingsland Road) yard, the engine going to St Philips Marsh shed. This return job also involved a 47XX Class engine.

Next on the list for road learning was from Didcot to Banbury. When I was learning this road I had several rides on the footplate of an express passenger between Oxford and Banbury. This express was the Pines. This train was now diesel-hauled and came from Bournemouth via Reading, and I could not help thinking of how different it was from when I first worked on this same train as a fireman 20 years previously.

This route learning was for the Channel Islands tomato traffic, so as to work it forwards from Westbury. Most of the traffic went towards the Midlands. We usually worked via

Newbury to Didcot, and then on to Banbury for relief with the trains going via Birmingham, but with the North of England and Scottish traffic we went through to Woodford Halse.

This train was operated with a Westbury-supplied engine, and after getting to Woodford we were booked to return to Westbury. We used to turn on a triangle on Woodford shed, and return light engine.

When working these trains we used to stop en route, somewhere between Westbury and Banbury to refill the tender with water. One day we had an excellent engine that was very light on using water. Everytime I mentioned taking water to my regular fireman he would say that we had enough water for Banbury. I also saw that we had a good supply. We had a good run, but on leaving Didcot, which was the last water column on the main line, we were stopped at nearly every signal for miles. This of course used a lot of water as we had to keep restarting the train. Eventually we were getting concerned about this extra water usage, and the supply was getting short. The next supply was at the water troughs at Aynho. Our supply had been used before we got to the troughs, but there was a good amount of water in the boiler. Onto the troughs we went with the scoop down and ready to pick up the much-needed water, but alas the troughs were dry. We dashed into Banbury goods loop with very little water to spare and refilled the tank with water as quickly as possible. It seemed ages before the water level indicator moved from zero, but with a sigh of relief order was soon restored. This incident was too close for comfort for my liking.

Another trip over this route was on a Saturday when we had to relieve a Weymouth to the Midlands express. We relieved the men at Westbury, and went via Swindon to Banbury with 5071 *Spitfire*, a 4-6-0 Castle Class. All went well until we were given "right away" from Oxford. We had just started when the brake was applied. The communication cord had been pulled. My regular fireman went back to meet the guard and to find out the cause of the trouble. In the coach where the cord had been pulled was an elderly lady who was very upset at having had to pull "The Cord". She explained that her husband had gone for a cup of tea. He was now dashing along the platform, with his two cups. He had gone into the buffet and had been left behind. The cord was reset and the guard asked my mate what he thought. My mate told him to forget it, as we would try to be in Banbury on time. We had a good run and arrived there near enough on time. No more was heard about this so no doubt the guard squared up the incident.

One day returning from Woodford light engine to Westbury, we were stopped at Hungerford and told that a London to the West of England express had not arrived at Bedwyn. The guard had been on the phone to Hungerford signalman but the engine had failed. We were told to go into the section, with the signalman's permission, to find the guard and train, and if possible to push the train out of the section. We went forward with caution, found the guard protecting the train, and took him to the train. The engine was a Western Class diesel. The driver saw me and asked us to couple up and push the train out of the section. This we did and put the train onto the up line at Bedwyn. A milk train which had been following could come alongside, and this engine could then be used to pull the failed engine and train to Westbury. We would then work the milk train to Westbury.

While waiting for the milk train to arrive I went up to the failed diesel and had a word with the driver. Diesels were new to everyone, and I knew nothing whatsoever of their workings. The driver mentioned that, although the engines were running he could not get any power to pull the train. "Is that what they call overspeed?" I asked. The driver dashed into the engine-room, and in a couple of minutes he returned and tried to get power, and was able to do so.

He whistled up and told everyone that he was now back in action and was all right to go. The signalman got all clear and with the guard's signal, away he went. All this happened before the milk train arrived. We were told to trail along behind, one section clear, in case he got into trouble again, but we saw no more of him. All I knew of diesels was what I had overheard when some of the senior drivers, who were being instructed on them at that time, were discussing these matters in the messroom. I found out later what caused the failure, but what I said seemed to have prompted the driver on how to put the job right.

One Monday morning we had to relieve a Taunton and Oxley goods at Westbury, and take it via Reading to Didcot. It was a Hall Class that had been a stand-by pilot at Taunton all the weekend. The fire had not been cleaned before being sent out on this trip. We started off up the Berks & Hants, but the engine was not very free for steam, as it had a dirty fire. We arrived at Reading but had to wait for relief for the guard. This was unfortunate as the fire got dull and lost most of its heat. When we did restart, the fire did not respond to its working condition and the engine would not steam. The coal on the tender was a lot of dead small and briquette dust. We could get no heat from the fire as it was lifeless; the flames were very short and were like gas jets. Although we were on the down relief line, there were no crossovers and no way out except to try and keep going to get to Didcot. We had to stop about four times in the 17 miles from Reading to Didcot and try to regain a little steam. When we got to Didcot the engine was changed, and we took it to the shed where it was reserviced.

Another night, we had a BR Standard Class 9F that had been stopped for repairs at Westbury. This engine had changed the one on the Taunton and Oxley which we had to relieve anyway. We started away, but before we got to Lavington the fireman, my regular mate, was in trouble with the firehole doors jamming, and steaming troubles. He was also never very happy to fire an engine left-handed. Being a genuine lad I offered to have a go at the firing and to try my luck. Although we managed to keep time and got to Didcot in good condition, the engine was not steaming very freely. We told the men of the situation, but they were confident that as we had done the hard bit from Westbury, they could manage the rest. Off they went, but the next day when they relieved us they said that they had not done too well for steam either. Our return working of this turn was to relieve a Didcot set at Foxhall Junction on a Banbury and Westbury freight, reforming the train at Swindon.

The return engine working from this Taunton and Oxley freight arrived in Didcot yard early in the morning, and was relieved by Westbury men who were booked to travel to Didcot via Swindon on a parcels train. After reforming the train we went back to Westbury via the Gold Coast. On arrival at Westbury the crew were relieved by Taunton men. Often the engine on this turn was 4985 *Allesly Hall*.

One day on the Woodford Purpot (the name given by railwaymen to a tomato special) we had a Westbury engine, No.4917 *Crosswood Hall*. This was a good engine. On returning back onto Westbury shed we were told that the engine had been withdrawn from service. Many other steam engines were being withdrawn in a similar manner to make way for diesel traction.

Road knowledge for this link still meant that I had to learn from Taunton to Newton Abbot, as well as the Cheddar Valley Branch from Witham Friary to Cheddar. This was done within a short time. The branch line turn was put into the link to keep it to full strength during the period when the specials were not running.

One trip that comes to mind was when we were booked to work an empty stock train from Heywood Road, en route from London to Newquay. We were to take it to Newton Abbot. Along came a 28XX with its empty coaches on. We relieved the men and off we went and took water on Fairwood troughs. On checking the weight of the train I found that we were overloaded for the Wellington bank. Water was again taken on at Creech troughs, so we did not stop at Taunton. We expected to find the Distant signal "on" for Wellington for us to stop, and allow a banker to get behind us. Alas the signal was "off", and we had a clear road. Consulting my regular mate I said: "What now?"; his reply was: "Have a go", so opening the regulator a bit more we gathered speed and sped through Wellington. At this speed we did not feel the weight of the train until we were most of the way up the bank and almost in sight of Whiteball Tunnel. I was then obliged to "drop the lever down" and to work the engine heavier. But the engine had the situation well in hand. We went on to Newton Abbot happily where we were relieved.

Going along the coast, from Dawlish Warren to Teignmouth was often not very comfortable during stormy weather between Dawlish station and the first tunnel. This was where the worst seas could be expected. At least twice my mate has been soaked with water from the rough seas coming over the sea-wall and spraying the engine with water.

A happier trip was when I was booked to conduct a works outing of Swindon factory workers on a Sunday going to Paignton, from Westbury to Newton Abbot and back. The train arrived at Westbury with 4079 *Pendennis Castle* in charge. Everything went according to plan, and we were relieved at Newton Abbot. I asked the Swindon men what they would like to do, as we were all booked to return with the same train during the evening. They told me that they would like to go on to Paignton and have a look around. They could then have a rest there. Arrangements were made, with a promise that we would relieve the return train on arrival at Newton Abbot that evening. This was done. On our return trip we had a good run. All the signals were at clear, and when we were passing Taunton we were signalled to use the through road. The speed over this route was 80mph and the speedometer needle sat on 80mph. The engine rode perfectly, and the track was like a billiard table. The engine had just been run in after having a general overhaul, and was a credit to all of the staff employed in the re-building of this engine. Many were, no doubt, passengers in this train.

One turn at Westbury was a petrol tank train from Fawley to Bromford Bridge (Birmingham). The engine was always a BR 92XXX 9F 2-10-0, and we used to relieve Salisbury men at Westbury, take the train to Bristol, there to be relieved by Bristol (Barrow Road, ex-LMS) men who then worked the train forward. Early one morning we relieved this train at Westbury and were told that the engine was not steaming very well and had made two unscheduled stops to get steam, and to refill the boiler. It was still in a sad state when we took over. At this late stage we could do nothing but carry on and try to get to Bristol. The Salisbury men said that they would tell the Control, who would make arrangements for a fresh engine from Bristol. Off we started, but my mate, although a good lad, did not make much headway in steaming this engine. When I offered to give him a spell and have a go this was readily accepted. I set about doing one or two things that I thought could get a result. We eventually got to Bristol without stopping and I managed to regain some of the lost steam pressure. Thinking that there would be a fresh engine waiting to change at Bristol, I was surprised that there was none. I asked the men, but they had received no message. I then told them of the non-steaming troubles, and that I had done the firing myself.

The driver, whom I had known from cleaning and firing days at Bath, knew that if I said that the engine was not steaming then that was good enough for him. The relieving fireman commented that "you Western people do not understand anything about these engines, we shall be all right". The other driver and I looked at each other, but made no comment. I wished them both the best of luck and off we went to get our return working.

The next day we were relieved again by the same men. They told us that they had taken several hours to get to Gloucester with this train. When we had left them the previous day the driver had told the fireman that he had personally known me for about 26 years, and being an ex-S&D man I had a fair idea of how to get an engine to steam.

One incident always brings a smile to my face when I recall the time when my mate was about to be going for his driving examination. He knew the routes as well as myself as we had been together for a long while and had been over these routes many times. I usually let him have a drive when we had a left-handed engine. One day from Westbury we were given a train for Severn Tunnel and beyond. The engine was a Stanier Black 5 so when we got aboard I decided to do the firing and let him have a drive. Having an idea that he would see how the engine would cope when going up Filton bank, and no doubt give me some work to do, I put the fire in order for this. As we started to climb the bank he began to work the engine heavier, and it responded as expected. I saw him look out of the corner of his eye to see what I intended to do, but taking no apparent notice I stayed sitting on the seat knowing that with what I had done the fire was in a fit state to deal with any kind of working that came its way.

Only once was I unable to complete the job and get home on a steam engine. This was on 6320, a 2-6-0 belonging to Westbury. We had relieved a Margam set at Severn Tunnel on a coal train for Salisbury. After a rough trip to Bristol we arrived at East depot, but I had given the Control advice that I was not prepared to take this train past Bristol East depot with this engine, and a fresh engine would be required. We were told to put the train off there and to go to Westbury light engine. We tried to do this, but on arrival at Bathampton loop, we had neither steam or water to go any further. I attempted to clean the fire while my mate went to the signalbox to tell everyone of our plight, and to make a can of tea. We still could not get any steam so I went to the signalbox, phoned Westbury Control, and asked for an assisting engine to pull us to Westbury. They were not helpful, so I phoned Bristol Control who sent a 42XX tank engine to pull us to Westbury. Eventually we arrived at about midnight where the engine was stopped for repairs. Several of the tubes were blocked, but the main cause of the engine not steaming was that the smokebox saddle seam had split. This was a Swindon factory job. Many of the staff thought that the engine would be withdrawn because of such a heavy repair, but no, it was put right, though it did not return to Westbury.

One night on the Taunton and Oxley freight we had this engine. Going over the Gold Coast we had a full load. There was a gale force wind blowing and the engine wheels could not get a grip onto the rails. We slipped to a standstill and had the greatest of difficulties in restarting the train. Soon all the sand was gone. When at last we got to Compton signalbox the Control wanted an explanation of what had caused our delay of about 30 minutes. When I explained the situation of the wind blowing the sand away from off the rails this was accepted. I never saw this engine again. It was withdrawn at Severn Tunnel Juntion at the end of 1963.

Many of the jobs that we worked with steam were now in the hands of diesels. The expresses that had been hauled by King Class and Castle Class were now dieselised. Shunting engines were now diesels, and many of the local passenger trains were DMUs. This left many of the goods, excursions and the assisting of overladen or underpowered diesel trains to the remaining steam engines.

Although I was in the group that were taught the diesel shunters, the 7000 (Maybach) Class, and the 800 (Warship) Class, our link was mostly still confined to steam.

On the Cheddar Valley goods job we took odd wagons of coal for different merchants to various wayside stations, tanks of bitumen to Cranmore for highway repairs, and empty wagons to quarries for stone. We picked up these empty wagons and tanks, and also the loaded stone wagons on our return trip. We went as far as Cheddar with this train.

One day on returning to Witham Friary we were asked by the Station Master if there was an empty van available on our train. There was, and as a van of tomatoes had been put off because it had a hot box they could make use of this van. Not only did we supply the van, but we all transhipped the vanload of tomatos, about 1,000 baskets, and took them to Westbury so that they could go on forward by a parcels train to catch the market the next day for where they were originally intended.

We also had a job where we went to Frome during the early morning with a rake of empty wagons for stone traffic. These we took to Frome Quarry sidings which is on the Radstock Branch, returning with a train load of stone. I did this job several times, but I never went any further towards Bristol than these quarry sidings. This job was always with a 57XX type Pannier Tank engine.

One Saturday evening early in 1963, we were booked on a spare turn. As it had been snowing heavily all day I wore Wellington boots to work. I thought that no doubt we would be called to take an engine with a steam lance fixed to the tube-cleaning lance cock and blow the snow clear of the points and crossings around Westbury station.

The foreman had other ideas. We were told to take a 22XX Class 0-6-0 to Witham Friary with shovels and get instructions from the signalman regarding assisting a local passenger train that was stuck in a snowdrift near to Wanstrow, on the Cheddar Valley line. We arrived at Witham Friary and got our orders to go into the section, find the train, and if possible to pull it back to Witham. We found the train, but it was in a snowdrift that came up to the footplate and above the bottom of the doors of the coaches. I walked through the snow to the engine, where I found the men. We decided that the best thing to do was to abandon the train, so I threw most of the fire out and made the engine safe. The engine was number 46527, a BR 2-6-0 Class 2MT. It would have been useless to have tried to free the train in this condition with our small engine. There were only two passengers in the two-coach set, so they were taken, with the train crew, back to Witham Friary, then to Frome, from where they had all originally set out. We returned to Westbury. The next day a breakdown gang and a gang of platelayers went to the train, and after several hours' work were able to get the train free of the snowdrift and take it to Frome.

After relieving a Bristol and Weymouth freight that left Westbury in the early afternoon, we were stopped at Sparkford and told to go into the up sidings as there were passenger trains approaching, one in each direction, and that Yeovil was not ready for us. Through the goods shed we propelled our train, and were pushing quietly towards the stop-blocks at less than walking pace. The guard was calling us back. As soon as he signalled us to stop I did so. No bump of impact was felt on the engine, but the guard walked behind the train where there should not have been any room. He reported to us that we had just touched these stop-blocks with his van, and that they had just simply collapsed. Of course all sorts of reports were soon flying around, but I heard little of this matter. I believe that the stop-blocks were never put back into position and the siding was soon taken out of use. Soon afterwards this section was made single-line track as were so many more sections in the modernisation of the railways.

During one of my spells of duty doing the foreman's job, I, as it were, "lost an engine". The engine Control asked me about an engine, a 28XX of 2-8-0 Class. It was reported to have worked into Westbury a few days previously and had not been listed as having worked away, or stopped for repairs. The problem was, where was it? I searched the engine lists but to no avail. Trying to gain a clue and discover where this engine could be, I walked around the shed, and much to my surprise there it was on the ash-pit road waiting to have the fire cleaned, and to refill the tender with coal. I asked the Westbury men, "What job are you on?" They said that they had called in to reservice the engine from the "Crookwood slip", a permanent way job, and were returning to the site when ready. The engine had been there for the last few days. I hurriedly let the engine Control know that I had found this engine. It was overdue for boiler washing-out and various examinations, so it had to go home without delay. It was worked home, and I supplied another engine for the engineering work. I had been called upon to do this office job for this day only, and as there was no entry made anywhere in respect of this engine being used for this or any other job, I was unaware of this move being made.

The Marlborough Branch, and the Cheddar Valley Branch line goods, along with the Frome Quarry stone working were all eventually diesel-hauled by a 7XXX Class Maybach. Several of the steam engines were dissapearing, and there were no more "Swindon trials" turns. Into our link came a turn of duty where we travelled to Swindon to prepare a passenger engine, usually a Castle Class, often 7037 *Swindon*, but then after a meal break took another engine to the goods yard to work a goods train back to Westbury, formerly the Trials goods turn. When returning from Bristol to Westbury with a freight train, instead of the normal 28XX or 72XX, we now often had a BR 92XXX or an LMS 2-8-0. I have even had an ex-LMS Class 5 type and a 70XXX Britannia on these trains. British Rail were slowly carrying out its modernisation programme.

Diesel engines were now to be recognised as the main form of power, and the remaining steam engines as the secondary source. There was an ever-increasing number of diesels being supplied to haul trains, but they were now going longer distances between reservicing. This and the closure of many small and branch-line stations meant that "railheads" were now being set up. This also meant that the small and many medium-size locomotive depots were either being closed, or were suffering a loss of work. It seemed that the idea was for the larger depots, such as Bristol, to have a large concentration of locomotive power, men, and work. This meant that these depots were in the best positions to be able to have one single maintenance staff to repair a fleet of diesels, and a greater flexibility of men and diesels could be made to deal with the work.

Wishing to return to Bath to live, and considering the situation that I thought was about to take place, I applied for a transfer to Bristol. For a number of years, Bristol had been served by two railway systems: the GWR who shedded their passenger engines at Bath Road and their goods engines at St Philips Marsh; and the LMS who shedded their engines at Barrow Road. Both systems mainly used Temple Meads station for passenger services. When diesels became the main power for passenger trains Bath Road shed was rebuilt to accommodate them. This left St Philips Marsh shed to deal with all the ex-GWR steam engines. All the ex-GWR train crews were now accommodated at Bath Road. Barrow Road meanwhile had several diesel turns. It was decided to tranfer the work, men, and diesels to Bath Road, and make Bristol into one large depot and amalgamate as one.

The next move was to put all the steam engines at Bristol onto Barrow Road shed. This was a good move as there was a better access, and a coal hopper, etc. St Philips Marsh steam shed was then closed.

Steam Twilight
at Bristol

After a few months I was notified that my transfer was to take place and I was to become one of the 535 drivers at Bristol. A great many of my former colleagues were at this depot. Many had transferred from Bath to get a driving job.

I had to learn several new sections of road. This tended to link up many of the sections that I had learnt while at Westbury. There was Bristol to Taunton, Swindon via Badminton, and Avonmouth via Henbury. Then Severn Tunnel to Cardiff, and of course all the goods yards and passenger coach sidings. I had also to revise Avonmouth via Clifton Down, Bath and Gloucester, where I had not been for several years. There were several new types of diesels that I had to learn to operate. After all this I was able to take my place in one of the numerous links of workings that existed at Bath Road.

For some while I did not get onto a steam engine, as there were several booked turns in this link for diesels only. When at last I did so it was to have a diesel one way and a steam engine the other way. These jobs were either to Swindon, Severn Tunnel or Gloucester.

According to an old note book that I have the turns that I did on steam engines towards the end of my working with steam were:

18-3-65	6815	Swindon - Bristol (11 vehicles - 248 tons)
28-4-65	6826	Light engine, Bath Road - Severn Tunnel
29-5-65	45272	Gloucester - Avonmouth - Barrow Road
15-6-65	92250	Barrow Road - East depot - Severn Tunnel
16-6-65	7029	(Clun Castle) - prepare on Barrow Road shed - take 92214 from Barrow Road to East depot - work to Severn Tunnel Junction.

Several more turns of a similar nature are recorded. I then came across the following sequence:

```
7-9-65    70053 Gloucester LMS - Mangotsfield - Barrow Rd
8-9-65    70045
9-9-65    70053
10-9-65   70045
11-9-65   70053
```

This was the same parcels job on all dates. The next steam turn was:-

```
13-9-65   6833 Gloucester - Bath Rd towing diesel D39
```

The following week came a turn where we had a diesel to Swindon and returned to Bristol with a goods train hauled by a steam engine. My notes read:

```
5-10-65   6923 Swindon - East depot - Barrow Road shed
6-10-65   6815
7-10-65   3863
8-10-65   (No Number)
9-10-65   6956 (all these were the same turn of duty)
```

I recall the last time that I worked a steam engine on a train to Exeter was one evening when we were spare. The foreman called for us and a guard to report to the office for his orders. He told us that the Branstone and Exeter coal train was on its way around towards the back of the shed (via St Philips Marsh) and we were to relieve the crew and take the train to Exeter. We waited at this point, but it did not appear. The time was getting on, so I asked the Control about the situation, and explained that we would like a clear run if possible so as to be able to get home from Exeter in good time. The train arrived with a Hall, and away we went. We did not stop anywhere until we arrived in the "laundry loop" at Exeter. The guard was an ex-S&D man, and we both knew each other's way of working. We did not exceed any speed limit for this coal train at any point. We had neither a jerk nor a snatch anywhere, and both agreed that it was an excellent trip. Taking the engine to the shed we were just in time to get the last passenger train home that night, known by railwaymen as the Northern.

One afternoon on a spare turn we were called, with a guard, to take a 92XXX that had been prepared, from Bath Road to Stoke Gifford, and from there to work a train of empties for the Midlands to Gloucester. Off we went and did the job as usual. About two days later I was told by an office clerk that the 92XXX Class engine that we had taken was the last steam engine owned by British Rail to leave Bath Road shed and work a train. There were a couple of steam engines that left the shed afterwards, but they went as light engines to other depots.

Steam traction had now ceased at Bristol and I never drove or fired a steam engine again, except once when I was invited to do so at one of the preserved steam railway sites.

My steam days were now at an end, as they were for so many of my work-mates. We were still travelling around the countryside and doing the same job, but with diesels.

I could not help but feel a little sad at the withdrawal of steam. I had spent 30 years working on steam, in which there was a certain pride in the job – the skill that was used as a fireman in getting the best possible results from the steaming qualities of the engine, and the skill as a driver when using these results to the best of one's ability in getting the train, as economically as possible, to its destination. Progress had arrived, and regretfully after so many years I had finished my Careering with Steam.